BILLIE HOLIDAY

BILLIE HOLIDAY

Chris Ingham

First published in the USA by Unanimous Ltd
254–258 Goswell Road, London EC1V 7RL

Series Editor: Martin Aston
Text Editor: Ian Fitzgerald
Project Editor: Nicola Birtwisle

ISBN: 1-56649-170-3

Distributed by Welcome Rain Distribution LLC

Printed in Italy

1 2 3 4 5 6 7 8 9

CONTENTS

ONE

THE STORY

The story of Billie Holiday, for many the greatest jazz singer of them all, is a story of conflict and contradictions. Brought up a staunch Catholic but compelled to satisfy a tremendous hedonistic appetite, she was – in the words of Catholic priest and Holiday enthusiast Peter O'Brien – a woman 'filled with a kind of joy of living and on the other hand tortured and disturbed'. She was a singer who was instinctive and unschooled, yet produced music of such remarkable melodic and particularly rhythmic sophistication that commentators and musicians continue to marvel. She remains a black female icon representing on the one hand a figure to aspire to – the noble, salty spirit of defiance in a racist world – and on the other a cautionary tale, a willing victim, a disheartening figure of dependency, hooked on narcotics, alcohol and abusive men.

There's joy here, and happy times, and great music, but following Billie as she careers through her forty-four years – getting some fun out of life whatever the cost – it's hard to share in the triumphs too heartily, framed as they often are in disaster. It's a story one hopes beyond reason will contain an escape off the destructive path, away from the inevitable spiral of hopelessness.

Details of Billie Holiday's early life were for years only available to us as mythologised tabloidese, as presented in her autobiography *Lady Sings The Blues,* ghosted by *New York Post* journalist William Dufty in 1956. Written during a vogue for sensational life stories as popularised by *True Confessions* magazine and movies such as *Love Me Or Leave Me* (Doris Day as driven-to-drink singer Ruth Etting) and *I'll Cry Tomorrow* (Susan Hayward as alcoholic actress Lillian Roth), the book had its eyes on Hollywood and served to perpetuate myths about Billie that were as difficult to disprove as they were to wholeheartedly believe.

The infamous opening lines set the tone. 'Mom and Pop were just a couple of kids when they got married. He was eighteen, she was sixteen, and I was three.' From that erroneous detail, the book moves swiftly on to grim, gripping accounts of family beatings; falling asleep in her Grandmother's arms before waking to find her dead while trapped in her stiff embrace; being raped aged ten by a 'Mr Dick'; being sent to a nun-supervised Catholic institution where she was locked in a room with a corpse; juvenile prostitution and predatory lesbians – one juicy, sordid scene after another. It was even hinted that the book only contained the milder material.

But even as the stories passed into legend, not helped by the 1972 film *Lady Sings The Blues* starring Diana Ross ('offensively simplified' said David Meeker in his book *Jazz In The Movies*), some commentators remained sceptical. Indeed, Holiday's 1975 biographer John Chilton sidestepped the difficulty of ascertaining the authenticity of the book's early details by concentrating his story on the period beginning with her first recording in 1933. Subsequent biographers Donald Clarke (*Wishing On The Moon*, 1994) and Stuart Nicholson (*Billie Holiday*, 1995) have gone to great trouble to excavate the facts and though some details remain unclear, it is from all these works that a consensus emerges.

Billie Holiday was born illegitimately as Eleanora Harris on 7 April 1915 at Philadelphia General Hospital. Though for some reason her eighteen-year-old mother Sadie registered the father's name as Frank De Viese, Sadie always told Eleanora that her father was Clarence Holiday, a Baltimore teenager who was in the army from 1917 to 1919 before adopting the life of an itinerant banjo player and guitarist, eventually settling in New York and establishing himself with Fletcher Henderson's orchestra between 1928 and 1933. Though Clarence seems to have helped out a little when he could, he didn't marry Sadie and there doesn't appear to have been any family life involving father, mother and daughter.

Moving back to Baltimore, where she was based, Sadie was often compelled to leave Eleanora with members of her family while she pursued employment, often out of town. The young-ster's formative years were spent in various households, some-times with her mother and latest husband (Sadie married Philip Gough in 1920, parting from him in 1923) or beau but more often elsewhere in the neglectful homes of members of Sadie's extended family. Inevitably, Eleanora reacted to this inattention by extensive truancy and was sent to Baltimore's Catholic-run House Of Good Shepherd For Colored Girls in 1925 to be stewarded by nuns, with the magistrate describing Eleanora as a 'minor without care and guardianship'. She was back in her mother's care after nine months.

Although the 'dead grandmother' and 'locked in with a corpse' stories remain unconfirmed, it is a matter of record that on 24 December 1926 one Wilbert Rich was arrested and charged with the rape of eleven-year-old Eleanora Gough (Eleanora had taken the name of Sadie's estranged husband.) Rich was sent to prison for three months while Eleanora was briefly sent back to the House Of Good Shepherd.

With her mother distracted by one more doomed love affair,

Eleanora found herself hanging around running errands for a local brothel, listening to the wind-up Victrola record player. It was here that she first heard the records that would change her life, music by blues singer Bessie Smith and jazzman Louis Armstrong, with one cut in particular – 1928's 'West End Blues' – making a profound impact upon her. Later, she was always quick to acknowledge the influence of both artists. 'I always liked the big volume and the big sound that Bessie Smith got when she sang,' she told an interviewer. She also added, 'I think I copied my style from Louis Armstrong.'

Her mother had moved to Harlem to seek work, leaving thirteen-year-old Eleanora to become a regular of Baltimore's nightlife – undoubtedly beginning her singing career in the bordellos of that city – before having her daughter join her in New York in early 1929. Their landlady there – Florence Williams – ran a whorehouse and with Sadie already working as a prostitute, it was not long before Eleanora joined her. Though her autobiography suggests she was turned in to the police for refusing to service a black customer ('Negroes would keep you up all the damn night handing you that stuff about "Is it good, baby?"'), it appears that there was a general raid on the house, with Eleanora among ten girls arrested and charged with vagrancy.

After four months in the hospital and workhouse, Eleanora rejoined her mother and they settled in Brooklyn, with Sadie getting domestic work and Eleanora determined never to hustle again or 'keep house for white folks'. She began singing with a neighbourhood saxophone player called Kenneth Hollon. They played at a few clubs for pennies thrown on the floor and Eleanora changed her name: to Billie, after her favourite film star Billie Dove, and Holiday after her father.

When her mother got a cooking job at Mexico's, a Harlem restaurant popular with musicians, Billie waited on tables and sang for tips. She was impressive enough to be asked to audition for Ed Small's Paradise, a 1,500-capacity night club, but came unstuck when asked what key she sang in and she didn't know. 'They shooed me out of there so fast, it wasn't even funny,' she recounted later.

She carried on singing, hung out with musicians, refused to collect tips using the traditional between-the-legs clip joint method (and got the sarcastic nickname 'Lady' from the other girls), then started appearing in some of Harlem's more popular bars and small clubs and slowly began to forge a reputation. The great bandleader and saxophonist Benny Carter remembered hearing her in the early 1930s and told Stuart Nicholson: 'she was not the typical blues singer...she was definitely not just another singer...I don't know if I ever heard anything prior to hearing her for the first time, or indeed since.' Billie hung out with Carter's band around 1932, joining in some of their after-hours jam sessions where guitarist Laurence Lucie remembered hearing in her 'a natural jazz feeling'.

British musician-writer Spike Hughes also saw her in a Harlem club around this time and paints a vivid picture: 'She was a tall, self-assured girl with rich, golden-brown skin, exquisitely shown off by the pale blue of her full-skirted and low-cut evening frock, her black swept-up hair and a pair of long, dangling paste earrings...like a gypsy fiddler in a Budapest cafe, she came over to your table and sang to you personally. I found her quite irresistible.'

He wasn't the only one. John Hammond, a Yale drop-out turned jazz writer-record producer-talent scout, turned up one night in early 1933 at Coven's, a small 132nd St club, expecting to hear Monette Moore, a favourite singer of his, but found she had been replaced by plump and vivacious Billie Holiday. He was amazed. Hammond contributed a regular column to the UK's *Melody Maker* and in April 1933 wrote: 'This month there has been a real find in the person of Billie Halliday [sic]... though only eighteen, she weighs over 200 pounds, is incredibly beautiful and sings as well as anybody I ever heard.' Later he recalled, 'she could take a tawdry tune and turn it around forty different ways. I never heard a singer who could do it this way.'

Bandleader-to-be and clarinettist Artie Shaw hung around Harlem in the early 1930s and was with pianist Willie 'The Lion' Smith when he heard Billie at the Catagonia Club on 133rd St, better known as Pod's And Jerry's (where, legend has it, she got the singing job by giving a lousy dance audition). 'She has a sense of time and a sense of phrasing that was jazz in the best sense of the word,' remembered Shaw. But Billie was making a bit of money and enjoying Harlem nightlife to the full and was already getting herself another kind of reputation, even at this early stage in her career. Shaw remembered: 'Willie said, she drinks too much and she gets fired from a lot of jobs. But she can sing.'

Hammond had taken clarinettist Benny Goodman to hear Billie and Goodman was impressed enough to date her while also agreeing to feature her on a Hammond-organised recording session in November 1933. Billie was terrified, not least due to the presence of Ethel Waters (a veteran singer who had already cut two numbers on the date and was checking out Hammond's latest discovery) and the huge microphone she had to sing into for the first time. 'Why do I have to sing into that thing?' she remembered thinking. 'I was scared to death of it.'

Although Billie eventually performed well on that Goodman date, she was not to record again for nearly two years (the affair over, Goodman hired Mildred Bailey for his next recording session). But several things of significance happened to her in the meantime. She began her first serious love affair, with pianist Bobby Henderson ('He was patient and loving: he knew what I was scared about and he knew how to smooth my troubles away,' she recalls wistfully in *Lady Sings The Blues*), ending it within a year when she discovered he was a bigamist. She also debuted at the famed Apollo Theatre, where she was so nervous she had to be literally pushed into the spotlight. Also, Hammond had got top impresario Irving Mills interested in representing her and he landed Billie an acting part in *Symphony In Black*, a Duke Ellington short in which she gives a remarkably mature and moving blues performance as a hard-done-by woman in love.

As well as being a persuasive example of Billie's early musical maturity, her appearance in *Symphony In Black* is a valuable and striking indication of her youthful physicality. In seeing it, we instantly understand the effect her presence would have had. Max Kaminsky, trumpeter and life-long friend, described seeing her in the mid 1930s: 'A large, fleshy, but beautiful boned woman, with satin-smooth beige skin. She had a shyness so vast, she spoke in practically a whisper. An uncompromising, devastatingly honest kind of girl, and always, in the deepest sense, a Lady.'

In 1934, she met a saxophonist, Lester Young, with whom she would have a durable, platonic, but deeply empathetic personal and musical relationship in the coming years. Young was the up-and-coming tenor saxophone stylist who was said to have 'cut' established sax stars Chu Berry and Coleman Hawkins and whose relaxed phrases and melodic interpretations were innately similar to, and certainly influential on, Billie's own evolving style. As well as shared enthusiasm for smoking marijuana, Billie and Lester appeared to be genuine soulmates. John Hammond witnessed this understanding between them and later commented that it was 'a relationship so subtle, so beautiful, it embarrasses me to even talk about it'.

Lester moved in with Sadie and Billie and expanded her existing nickname, calling her 'Lady Day' and her mother 'Duchess'. She in return named him The President of the Saxophone or Pres: 'the top man in this country,' as she believed he was.

In 1935, John Hammond was able to secure a record deal for Teddy Wilson, a remarkably gifted pianist he had been promoting around town for the last year. The boom in the jukebox business meant Brunswick records were prepared to sign Wilson (with Hammond as producer) to record a session a month for a year. Although the budget was tight, top players would still work for union scale during The Depression and Hammond was able to hire quality small groups to play Wilson's sketched arrangements, as well as give his favourite singer her next break.

The resulting session on 2 July 1935 began a series of historic recordings with Wilson that would last until early 1939 and would form the foundation of Billie Holiday's reputation as arguably the greatest small-group jazz singer of all time. The combination of Wilson's irreproachably elegant, cascading piano, the infectious two-beat swing feel, the greatest soloists of the time and Billie's grainy-toned, rhythmically audacious vocals also put the recordings among the best jazz of the era.

There are songs from this period that remain famous as standards ('These Foolish Things', 'I Can't Give You Anything But Love', 'He's Funny That Way', 'The Very Thought Of You', a clutch of Gershwins, a handful of Kerns) and others that have become particularly synonymous with Billie Holiday ('What A Little Moonlight Can Do', 'My Man', 'Billie's Blues', 'Mean To Me'). Yet there are many obscure, short-lived compositions that, in spite of the often spirited, not to say inspired performances they receive, hardly seemed worth the effort to some commentators. Teddy Wilson recalled that they often had to select tunes from publishers that other, better-established artists had already rejected. Wilson said: 'In those days the publishers made the hits. They had what they called number one, number two and number three plugs – the songs they were pushing. We never got into the plug tunes, we had our choice of the rest. That's why many of those songs we recorded, you never heard anybody singing besides Billie.'

Teddy Wilson confirms that the first Wilson–Holiday session had somehow captured an early magic. 'That session was never, never surpassed,' remembered Wilson. 'It may have been equalled, but never surpassed.' The initial reaction to Billie Holiday's singing was guarded, however. Brunswick executives were disappointed that she didn't sound more like Cleo Brown (a popular singer of the day) and that audiences at the Apollo saved their demands for encores for other performers, and Billie was actually replaced at the Famous Door club after four nights in favour of showier entertainment.

However, towards the end of the year the Wilson–Holiday sides were Brunswick's best-sellers, and over the coming months Mills got her some lucrative work, including a week in Montreal, a spot in the Louis Armstrong-led revue *Stars Over Broadway* and a tour with Jimmie Lunceford's Orchestra. But that didn't prevent Billie signing up with Louis Armstrong's hustling agent-manager Joe Glaser, who promptly put in her the Grand Terrace, Chicago, with Fletcher Henderson's Orchestra. She got good reviews – 'you can't help but go for Billie Holiday songs,' said *New York Age,* commenting on a radio broadcast – but she fell foul over the Terrace's owner Ed Fox, who didn't like Billie's style, saying, as he fired her, 'everyone says you sing too slow. Get out!' (so Billie remembered). Glaser agreed with Fox, as Billie recalled: 'You gotta speed up the tempo, you gotta sing hot stuff,' to which Billie remembered replying, 'Look, you son-of-a-bitch, you sing it. I'm going to sing it my way, you sing it your way.'

9

There was more trouble at the Onyx club where she clashed with headliner violinist Stuff Smith who took exception to what he thought was Billie's 'milking' of the applause, and she was fired at Smith's request. Clearly doing something right, however, one year and twenty Teddy Wilson sides into her proper recording career, Billie was offered a contract of her own with Vocalian, a subsidiary of Brunswick. Billie always credited the influence of songwriter and current lover Bernie Hanighen for that significant break, and the recordings issued as by 'Billie Holiday And Her Orchestra' were produced by Hanighen himself and were often on an artistic par as those issued by 'Teddy Wilson And His Orchestra', upon which Billie continued to appear.

In February 1937 Clarence Holiday, Billie's father, died aged 38 from influenza, possibly aggravated by a wartime gassing. Billie was shocked by the news, even though they had never been close. When Billie had started appearing on the New York scene where he was established, he was anxious not to be perceived as old enough to be father to a girl the same age as those he was trying to attract and kept her at a distance. Equally, when Billie was in a position to hire musicians, she never got round to using Clarence, which apparently stung him. The funeral was dramatic. Sadie lost her way to the church, missing the interment; Clarence's new wife, along with his mistress and two of Clarence's children by her, were also there.

When with certain musicians, Billie would sit them down with some brandy and ask about her father. Trombonist Floyd Brady, who played with Clarence and later, in 1945, with Billie, recalls how tickled she would be to be told 'he was the tops, a great musician, and having you around is living proof of his greatness.'

Between March 1937 and February 1938, Billie sang with the hard-swinging Kansas City band led by Count Basie. She had already recorded one of her great sessions with some key Basie-ites (including Lester Young and trumpeter Buck Clayton) in early 1937 and John Hammond had persuaded Basie that a female singer was just what the band needed to overcome the resistance they had felt away from their home town. Basie, like so many others, was struck. 'I was really turned on by her,' he told biographer Albert Murray. 'A very, very attractive lady. And when she sang, it was an altogether different style. I hadn't heard anything like it and I was all for it.'

At one of her first engagements with the band, at the Apollo Theatre, Billie – with a customised song selection of her own – stole the show. '[She] sure was a big help to us on that program,' admitted Basie. 'She fitted in so easily, it was like having another soloist.' The band hit the road for a series of one-nighters and though Billie was no lover of road life, she was surrounded by pals. Hanging out with Lester and Buck – they called themselves the Unholy Three – she was also having an affair with guitarist Freddie Green. Saxophonist Earle Warren remembered, 'Billie, like Lester, was always jovial and entertaining, very seldom moody and obstinate.' Trumpeter Harry 'Sweets' Edison concurred: 'It would be most beautiful the whole trip, because everybody loved Lester and everybody loved Billie.'

However, clearly not everybody loved what was perceived as a less-than-rigorous approach to the job of singing and after eleven months Billie was sacked. Basie is diplomatically vague in his memories ('I think Billie left because she got the chance to make more money'), but Billie herself remembered refusing to sing blues and rowing with John Hammond because of it. Band manager Willard Alexander was categorical in a 1938 interview with *Down Beat* magazine: 'The reason for her dismissal was strictly one of deportment, which was unsatisfactory, and a distinctly wrong attitude to her work. Billie sang fine when she felt like it. We just couldn't count on her for consistent performance.'

Basie's loss was Artie Shaw's gain. A long-time admirer of Billie's talent, the swing visionary lost no time in hiring her in March 1938. 'The minute Billie came in the band the guys could hear the difference in the way she hit a song,' Shaw recalled. 'Naturally, they had a lot of respect for her musically.' Of course Shaw's orchestra being an all-white band meant hiring a black female singer was not going to make it easy for anyone, but Shaw and Holiday considered it to be society's problem, not theirs. Shaw said: 'People used to say "why did you hire her?" and I used to say "she was the only singer around who could keep up with that band".'

The notices were excellent. 'Whatever you do, don't miss Billie Holiday with Art Shaw's band,' raved one; 'the addition of Billie Holiday to Shaw's band has put this outfit in the top brackets,' gushed another. Billie was as stubborn on repertoire as ever, which suited Shaw who had an antipathy toward the Tin Pan Alley plugs of the day, but it was not long before Shaw was under pressure to hire a white singer to satisfy pluggers and ballroom bookers.

The routine racism that Billie and the band encountered was greeted with good humour at first. Billie tells the story of betting members of the band that a sheriff in the southern states would slur her before too long. When he did ('Hey you! What's Blackie going to sing?') and Artie blanched, she laughed out loud and collected the money. But the grinding monotony and sheer inconvenience of the prejudice (several refusals in hotels and restaurants, trying to find a bathroom, often being unable to sit on the stage when not singing) began to wear Billie down. Southern dates were particularly unpleasant. One date had a member of the audience cheering for the 'nigger wench' to sing another song. 'He didn't mean it,' remembered Shaw, 'he meant she sounds good, we like her'. Billie did not see it that way and mouthed 'Motherfucker' at the man, before being escorted quickly away from the venue as pandemonium erupted.

Disliked by publishers, 'rested' by radio, described by even Shaw's management as 'too artistic', Billie's role in the band was marginalised to such an extent that she found herself sitting alone upstairs in a hotel before coming down to sing one or two numbers. There was contract wrangling too. Shaw had signed with Victor but Billie was still contracted to Vocalian – hence their one side together, the Shaw-written 'Any Old Time' was quickly withdrawn. Also, Shaw apparently wanted Billie to sign to him for five years, which she refused to do. The final straw, however, was when the orchestra was appearing at the Lincoln Hotel, New York, and the manager asked Artie to instruct Billie to use the back entrance and freight elevators and to stay out of public areas in the hotel. By November 1938, Billie Holiday was no longer with Artie Shaw.

There were recriminations in the music press, the black press and even the popular Walter Winchell column in the *Daily Mirror*, and Shaw was forced to defend himself against charges of racism, accusations that still made him angry when talking to Stuart Nicholson in 1993. 'They said I fired her because she was black, conveniently overlooking that when I hired her she was black too! I've even been castigated for hiring her – I was told I was exploiting a black person. I was not exploiting her. I was doing the best I could to present her in an impartial light as a musician singing in my band. No matter what I do, it seems I'm wrong!'

Holiday allowed affectionate words about Shaw into her autobiography ('He's a wild one; he has his own peculiarities but he's amazing and a good cat deep down') while Shaw in later years was quick to take opportunities to pay tribute to

Billie, particularly her strength and pride: 'She had reason to have pride, she was a hell of a singer.'

Relations with John Hammond had become awkward since the Basie days – there had been disagreements about repertoire and Hammond was irritated and perturbed by her need to get high on recording sessions – and he even omitted her from the bill of his famous 'From Spirituals To Swing' concert at Carnegie Hall in December 1938 before finally ending his association with her career after a January 1939 recording session.

A few weeks earlier, however, Hammond had once more been responsible for an important break in Billie's fortunes. Barney Josephson – an out-of-town businessman with what he described as a 'democratic upbringing' – opened the Café Society, New York's first racially integrated supper club. Determinedly liberal and gently mocking the night-loving socialites of the club scene, Josephson delighted in making the Café Society's slogan 'The Right Place For the Wrong People'. Hammond organised the entertainment, hiring a band based around trumpeter Frankie Newton plus boogie pianists Albert Ammons and Meade Lux Lewis with Billie as featured artist. Both the club and Billie were a huge hit and Billie's performing confidence grew: 'she really flowered', remembered Josephson.

With her repertoire and performance character becoming more and more focused on the unlucky-in-love theme, Billie was initially unsure of a song offered to her by poet Abel Meeropol, who wrote under the name of Lewis Allen: a startling, painfully vivid depiction of lynching victims called 'Strange Fruit' in which the 'fruit' are Negro corpses dangling from poplar trees. 'What do you want me to do with that, man?' Josephson remembers her saying upon hearing it. By the time she had heard it a few times, however, she was determined to sing it.

Placed at the end of her set, 'Strange Fruit' became a

forbidding, compelling piece of theatre. Josephson arranged for the lights to be dimmed to a single spot and the waiters to cease serving while Billie delivered the harrowing number to a rapt club. Following the final line – 'Here is a strange and bitter crop' – darkness fell upon the club and when the lights came back up, Billie had gone. With Josephson insisting on no encore to disturb the poignancy, the moment electrified the club night after night.

It must have been an amazing, incongruous moment to have this transfixing tale of extreme racial violence performed for a nightclub audience. 'It was unforgettable,' remembered Josephson. 'I listened to it three times a night; she sang it every set. I made her do it as her last number…When she sang "Strange Fruit" she never moved. Her hands were down. She didn't even touch the mike…the tears would come and just knock everybody in that house out.'

We can get some idea of Billie's physical way with the song from the January 1959 TV recording she did in London. Standing still and shot close to her face, we can see how the loll of her head, the movement of her eyes and eyebrows, the expression of her mouth between phrases which, while registering gentle disgust for what she is singing about, also conveys a sad determination to say what has to be said – 'if I can go through this, you certainly can'. All this physical detail contributes immeasurably to the impact of her performance. Billie Holiday was a great actress.

Not everyone appreciated what 'Strange Fruit' achieved, either for Billie as an artist or as entertainment in general. John Hammond made no secret of his distaste for the song, citing it as the moment Billie became less jazz singer, more *chanteuse* locked into doomy ballads about pain, loss and hopelessness. Some patrons walked out on the song and one customer – who had witnessed a lynching as a child – followed Billie into the powder room, saying 'don't you ever sing that song again'. One can see their point: it would be hard to go back to your cocktails after having stark images of twisted mouths and burning flesh sung at you.

Others missed the point completely. Billie tells the story (in *Lady Sings The Blues*) of one night in Los Angeles when 'a bitch stood up in the club I was singing and said, "Billie, why don't you sing that sexy song you're so famous for? You know, the one about the naked bodies swinging in the trees".'

Such was the power of the song that Billie's picture appeared in *Time-Life* magazine – thought by Josephson to be the first black face to appear in the publication. Billie, for her part, grew more and more involved in the song, with the intensity of the lyric and her performance often moving her to tears.

Still recording with the same company but now on the Columbia label (the Vocalian label had recently been purchased by Decca), Billie was dismayed when they would not record 'Strange Fruit'. She approached Milt Gabler, owner of the independent jazz record company Commodore Records. He was given permission by Columbia to borrow Billie for one session, and released 'Strange Fruit' coupled with an original blues called 'Fine And Mellow'. It was a hit and with the ensuing controversy, Billie began enjoying her first wave of attention from outside the exclusive circle of musicians and jazz lovers.

Billie's initial stay at the Café Society lasted until August 1939, but when returning in November of that year she was offered better money to go to Ernie's (a club in the village) that Josephson would not match and she quit. Following Ernie's there was an extended stay at Kelly's Stables on 52nd Street with trumpeter Roy Eldridge. 'She seemed to have such a rapport with people,' recalled Eldridge, 'man, she was out of sight'. The next couple of years saw Billie in high-profile engagements at the Apollo, the Famous Door and back at the

Café Society. 52nd Street had a war-time boom, with clubs benefiting from the military on leave and with Billie a mainstay of the scene (she was sometimes billed 'Queen Of 52nd Street'), she continued to build a reputation among the cognoscenti. However, the wider appeal she confessed to desiring persisted in eluding her.

Billie had a lusty, promiscuous love life with a string of care-free affairs (several musicians, fans and even the occasional music journalist were among her beaus) interspersed with seri-ous attachments. Billie's engagement to pianist Sonny White had been announced in mid-1939, though by the end of the year the relationship had run its course, Billie saying 'like me, he lives with his mother, our plans for marriage didn't gel'. Someone who did not live with his mother and who dazzled Billie in early 1940 was hipster hustler Jimmy Monroe. Both Billie's mother and manager Joe Glaser warned her against Monroe but despite them – perhaps even as the autobiography suggests, to spite them – Monroe and Billie were married in August 1941. Before they split up in 1943 Monroe had man-aged to spend Billie's by now regular and substantial earnings on good times and lawyers (he was arrested in 1942 for drug smuggling), introduced her to opium-smoking and probably inspired one of Billie's famous tunes, 'Don't Explain', with his infidelity and brutality. And pianist Jimmy Rowles thought Monroe 'wasn't too bad' when compared to some of the other men in Billie's life.

The unreliability that had aggravated and ultimately alienat-ed John Hammond became even more pronounced as Billie suc-cumbed to what would be a more or less life-long addiction to hard drugs. Billie had always consumed alcohol and marijuana with relish, but with her higher-profile bookings, clubs were taking her attitude more seriously, sometimes capping her wages as an insurance against her unpredictability. But Billie had to get high and heroin was the hippest, happiest high of them all.

Some regarded her impulsive attitude affectionately, an inextricable part of what made her unique. Bass player at the Café Society John Williams remembered: 'She did what she liked. If a man came up she liked, she'd go with him; if a woman, the same thing. If she was handed a drink, she'd drink it. If you had a stick of pot, she'd take a cab ride in the break and smoke it. If you had something stronger she'd use that. That was her way. She didn't apologise for it and she didn't feel ashamed...she had a real zest for life.'

Of course this zest, coupled with her temperamental approach to business and an uncompromising approach to her art (Frank Sinatra, who adored her work, told her 'Lady, you're not commercial'), were exactly the restrictions that precluded Billie enhancing her appeal. Being who she was, concessions to the straight white world were out of the question.

This attitude undoubtedly contributed to Columbia refusing to renew Billie's contract, and in February 1942 Billie recorded her final session for the company. She continued to work regularly though *Down Beat* had been keeping a wary eye on recent shows, reviewing Billie's performance at the Onyx on 52nd Street (where she played through most of 1943 and 1944) thus: 'Billie is not singing at her best in our opinion, nor does she sing often enough.'

In March 1944 (following the American Federation Of Musicians' recording ban of July 1942–September 1943) Billie was back recording on Milt Gabler's Commodore label along with the Café Society band and the music was discernably smoother. 'She wanted to really be a pop singer,' remembered Gabler. 'This was the start of her having a non-jazz background.'

When Gabler heard her singing 'Lover Man', a song written by Jimmy Davis and pianist Roger 'Ram' Ramirez, he was very enthusiastic. 'Lover Man' was a frankly sensual song of desire that was having some success being sung by gay Billie imitator Willie Dukes. When Billie decided to feature it herself, 'that gave it the carte blanche,' remembered Ramirez. 'Those were lurid and sexy lyrics for the time, "You'll make love to me"... In those days it was a no-no.'

'I said to myself "Smash hit! I got to record that",' remembered Gabler, finding himself in a dilemma. Since 1941, he had been an A&R man at Decca Records and was only permitted to continue with Commodore with a proviso. 'If I record it for Commodore, Jack Kapp [president of Decca] will fire me because he allowed me to record Commodore records as long as I stuck to jazz and didn't make pop hits.'

So Gabler signed her to Decca and Billie, perhaps seeing her chance to establish her star credentials – in attitude, if not quite yet in name – asked for strings as a backing, a luxury afforded to only the top stars. Gabler agreed and booked Decca's musical director, ex-Jimmy Dorsey reedsman 'Toots' Camarata, to arrange her first session on 4 October 1944. 'She came into the studio, turned around and walked right out!' remembered Camarata. 'I went after her and asked her what was wrong. She said "Oh man, those strings hit me pretty hard."' Picking up a bottle of cherry brandy from a nearby liquor store, Camarata and Billie cut 'Lover Man' and a Camarata original called 'No More'. 'The date went quite smoothly as I recall,' said Camarata.

The strings were a deft move that served to distinguish Billie's current recording activities from the small jazz group achievements of the Columbia years and were a concerted effort to commercialise her appeal. This delighted Gabler, who always wanted to present Billie as a pop singer. 'To me, she used to sing in clubs for losers...But I wanted to project these ballads as songs. I was always a song man.'

Billie's and Gabler's instincts were right. The string-laden 'Lover Man' was a national hit and Billie's star began to rise.

Toward the end of the Columbia period, Billie's name had started appearing on the occasional composition credit including 'Tell Me More And More, And Then Some' credited solely to B. Holiday. However, friend and lyricist-composer Arthur Herzog remembers himself and his friend Danny Mendelsohn being asked by Billie to 'take down' a 'great tune' she had in her head. 'Yes, Billie, it's a great tune,' Herzog remembers Mendelsohn saying, 'but it's "St James' Infirmary". They 'bent it' on Billie's instructions and forgot about it until seeing the credit months later. 'Danny, what are we going to do about this?' Herzog remembers saying. 'This idiot friend has done this to us and the song isn't worth a goddamn.'

Another Holiday composition co-credit is 'God Bless The Child', an affectingly rational piece about independence, survival of the fittest, the transitional nature of money and the limitations of familial ties that remains one of Billie's most famous songs. The story goes that she had a row with her mother who, despite being on the receiving end of Billie's generosity many times, would not lend her some money when she needed it. Billie brooded about it for three weeks until 'One day a whole damn song fell into place in my head.' She ran round to Herzog and dictated it to him: 'we changed the lyrics in a couple of spots, but not much,' said her autobiography.

Herzog remembers it differently. He recalls asking Billie for a down-home Southern expression he and Danny Mendelsohn could construct a song around, and upon getting it, claimed to write it himself in twenty minutes, dictating it to Mendelsohn. 'Billie said "I want to do it this way",' remembered Herzog, 'and we changed one note a half a tone...I said "Billie, I'll give you half the song if you make the record."' Herzog is categorical: 'She has never written a line of words or music,' maintaining that Billie was 'a great artist, but creative – no'.

A significant record of the Decca period was the Holiday-Herzog credited 'Don't Explain', one of Billie's legendary story-of-my-life songs. In *Lady Sings The Blues* she tells of falling out with husband Jimmy Monroe who had returned one night with another woman's lipstick on his collar. 'Take a bath, man,' Billie remembers saying, 'don't explain'. Thinking about turning 'an ugly scene into a sad song' and 'singing phrases to myself...suddenly I had a whole song'. Herzog, who is co-credited, may well have had a different story, but this time he did not tell it.

Meanwhile, Billie's latest unfortunate choice of man was trumpeter, heroin-user and -supplier Joe Guy. In a not untypical moment of wishful thinking, Billie announced her divorce from Monroe (he had been arrested for drug smuggling again) and her marriage to Guy, though in fact neither took place. Billie indulged Guy's ambitious plans for a big band and invested large amounts of money on uniforms, arrangements and other cash-draining aspects of the project. Billie and Guy took the band on the road in September 1945 but about a month into the band's first series of one-nighters, news came to Billie of her mother Sadie's death.

Although theirs was often a troubled and confused mother-daughter relationship, they had been through a lot together since the move to New York in 1929, inspiring a certain tempestuous closeness, and Billie was devastated. It was thought by some that she never really recovered from the loss. Certainly she lost all interest in going on the road with Guy's band – eventually having to foot a reputed $35,000 bill for the folded venture – and there were reports of an intensifying drug and alcohol dependency with attendant erratic performances and behaviour. Lady had changed.

Ralph Watkins, who had run Kelly's Stable in the early

1940s, noticed the difference in Billie when he returned from the military in 1945. 'She was on a very expensive habit. By then she never had enough money, no matter how much she made. She was borrowing all the time. She was making over a thousand a week.'

Her conduct on recording sessions was becoming erratic. Bassist and ex-lover John Simmons was present on one Decca session and remembered Billie's behaviour. 'She'd take time out between records to go in the ladies room, to get herself together. She'd be in there an hour, an hour and a half. People were pulling out their hair, it was like money running out their pockets.' At the peak of her commercial powers and with a sympathetic record company pulling for her, it was not a good time to be carrying a heroin habit.

Her increasingly unpredictable demeanour notwithstanding, Gabler remembered Billie as 'basically a one-take artist'. The problem in this period was getting her ready to work. 'Sometimes when I would record her, I would have the band all rehearsed,' remembered Gabler, 'and Billie would come in from the other studio where she had been relaxing. While she was in there, I'd send a runner out to get a bottle of brandy to clear her throat.' Her then-pianist Bobby Tucker remembers getting her to a midday session at 2.30pm. 'The orchestra had been rehearsing, and the sound man had the balance correct and they were figuring, "Well, this one is on the house". But Lady came in, and we were through at ten minutes to three. And I don't think we did a double take on any of them.'

Billie's career was at a peak. Her new orchestrated recordings direction on Decca was proving popular with record-buyers and critics alike. Even the jazz press was far from discouraging about what they heard. 'Billie has never been in better voice or better accompanied than on these sides,' said *Metronome* of a mid-1945 session, 'we're enthusiastic about the continued use of strings as a setting for her voice.' She started playing concert halls, including being part of a recital in February 1946 at Philadelphia's Academy Of Music, and her solo concert debut the same week – 'a major event in the jazz world' as the programme notes said – at New York's Town Hall.

The Town Hall concert was a triumph, the *New York Times* calling her singing 'pure enchantment' and another review contrasting the performance to her unpredictable club appearances. 'Gone was the moodiness...the reluctance to perform that have often made her a singer with no real love of her work,' wrote Seymour Peck. 'She was glad to be singing, perhaps no less than her audience was to be hearing her.' Three months later she appeared at Carnegie Hall with Norman Granz's touring 'Jazz At The Philharmonic' presentation (a popular attempt to bring the excitement of the jazz club jam session to the concert hall) to a rousing reception.

It was perhaps the taste of popular success that inspired her to swallow her racial pride and accept a part as a maid in the Hollywood version of the story of jazz, *New Orleans*. ('She's a cute maid,' she told Leonard Feather in hopeful justification of what he thought a demeaning compromise.) Also featuring Billie's idol Louis Armstrong (as a butler) – another inducement to be involved, undoubtedly – the film itself is bland and conventional (its noble intentions apparently compromised by McCarthyist pressure) but the musical sequences are valuable visual documents of Billie at her commercial peak.

Her drug habit was contributing to continued unreliability, however. Joe Guy had tried to supply Billie in Hollywood on the set of *New Orleans* and Joe Glaser attempted some damage limitation by having him banned from the studio. But, naturally, this protection could only be temporary. There followed erratic performances and costly, unproductive recording sessions. Sensing a situation spinning out of control, Glaser threatened the withdrawal of his managerial services, forcing Billie to check in to hospital in March 1947 to kick the habit once and for all. She agreed to a six-week stay in a private Westchester clinic. Three weeks after leaving the clinic on 19 May 1947 she was arrested in New York for possession of heroin.

The circumstances were bizarre. Billie had been playing in Philadelphia and returned to her hotel after the final show, waiting in the car while her pianist Bobby Tucker and road manager Jimmy Asciendo returned to the room to retrieve their things. The hotel had been under surveillance by the Federal Bureau of Narcotics whose agents asked to search the room, finding heroin capsules wrapped in a stocking under the bed. The entirely innocent Tucker and the probably not-so-innocent Asciendo were arrested and Billie somehow got back to New York (driving herself for the first time ever, pulling away in a 'hail of bullets' if one believes the autobiography), eventually being arrested along with Joe Guy three days later.

While it is clear that Billie was using heroin at this time, there was barely a legal case against her (or Guy) in this particular instance – there was certainly nothing to link her directly to the evidence. However, in a decision that would cost her dearly but which was perhaps taken in an effort to grasp a genuine opportunity to get clean, Billie chose to waive her right to legal representation and pleaded guilty, asking to be taken to hospital. To her dismay she was convicted as a felon and sentenced to a year and a day in prison.

It has been suggested that Joe Glaser – in his determination to get her off drugs and away from Joe Guy – was culpable in both the arrest and disastrous legal outcome of Billie's trial. Certainly he was elusive when, while quietly doing her time, Billie wrote (with the help of warden and friend Helen Hironimous) to ask for money and a statement of account.

Glaser eventually responded to say Billie owed him $715, adding 'It is a pity what she did with about $100,000 she made in two and a half years but that is exactly what happened during her association with Joe Guy.' Norman Granz organised a benefit concert knowing Billie was broke but Glaser – not wanting Billie's destitution to become known – refused the money on her behalf and the funds raised were donated to charity.

Hironimous was outraged by Glaser's apparent callousness and persuaded Billie to change agencies (to Ed Fishman's West Coast operation) and even had Billie consent to a further three months custody, beyond when she was due for parole, better to ensure a full cure. Billie was released on 16 March 1948 to find both Fishman and Glaser hustling for commission on her 27 March comeback concert at Carnegie Hall, promoted by Ernie Anderson. Not only did Billie decide to revert to Glaser as manager, she was also temporarily reunited with husband Jimmy Monroe. Billie's life never became quite different enough to escape the old dangers.

The Carnegie Hall concert was an emotional and triumphant return that broke box office records, with a hastily arranged second concert three weeks later breaking the record again. There was undoubtedly a prurient aspect to this audience interest ('They come to see me get all fouled up, just waiting for that moment. But they're not going to get it,' Billie complained to *Metronome* later) but there seemed to be genuine warmth in the reception the audience gave her and Billie responded by singing twenty-one songs and six encores.

Pianist Bobby Tucker remembers it as one of the highlights of his life. 'She did one helluva show. It was fantastic. It was unbelievable. There were seats in the aisles, and there were about six hundred people sitting on the stage…There were people sitting around the piano, it was like a living room.'

Many commentators noticed how well she looked and how happy she seemed.

The reality of having a criminal conviction, however, meant Billie was denied a Cabaret Card which meant she could not work anywhere where alcohol was sold, including in New York clubs. So, alternative contexts were arranged, including the jazz revue *Holiday On Broadway* at the Mansfield Theatre – which confused the critics but delighted audiences – and a sixteen-week run with the Count Basie Orchestra. In May, however, Billie did appear at a club; four weeks at Club Ebony with the Cabaret Card problem 'arranged' by co-owner John Levy. Levy went all out – gowns, furs, a Cadillac – to become Billie's new man and it was not long before Billie was telling *Ebony* magazine, 'I never do anything without John telling me.'

Though she also told *Ebony* that she preferred a man 'to be dominating at all times', Levy's brand of dominating was pretty extreme. He controlled all Billie's finances, forcing her to ask for spending money, and played psychological games to affect her performance. Pianist Horace Henderson witnessed it: 'he always made a habit of making her mad five minutes before she got ready to perform,' Henderson remembered, 'she would go on stage with tears in her eyes and give one of the best performances.' Pianist Jimmy Rowles said Levy actually beat Billie up before performances with the effect of making the delivery of 'victim' songs like 'My Man' and defiant songs of individual choice like 'T'aint Nobody's Business' all the more authentic. Rowles said: 'If she aches, it's great, she's happy; if he kicks her good, she can sing.'

Rowles was not the only one to observe that Billie 'was unfortunate enough to be mentally arranged that she had to have a cat that beat the shit out of her three times a week to keep her happy'. A boyfriend from the mid-1940s, bassist John Simmons, was categorical: 'She was a masochist. She was doing things to make me fight her.' Simmons bought a cat-of-nine-tails: 'I caught her with this whip...I hit her everywhere but in her face and the bottom of her feet...Never fazed her.'

Levy was described by his ex-wife as 'a miserable bastard, a terrible man' and by pianist Bobby Tucker as 'doing the business on both sides of the law' and 'a pimp, an awful person'. But he was Billie's man and she stuck with him for a difficult couple of years as she criss-crossed the country, finding alternatives to working in New York clubs.

There was little doubt that Billie had gone back on drugs – some thought by as early as the second Carnegie Hall concert, four weeks after her release – and it was not long before her old unreliability surfaced again, to her immediate cost. She failed to show at the first post-prison recording session arranged for her by Decca on 22 October 1948, with the result that the entire session was billed to Billie's royalty account.

Billie received more damaging publicity. In January 1949 a fracas in the kitchen of Los Angeles club Billy Berg's – in which Billie accused someone of molesting her and John Levy waded in with a knife while Billie threw plates and screamed – resulted in three people being hospitalised and two people, Levy and Billie, arrested. Within three weeks, she was arrested again for possession of opium.

This time Billie took counsel and was advised to detoxify and allow herself to be tested. With several judiciously arranged adjournments and delays, Billie was finally found not guilty in May 1949, but not before she had fallen into anxiety and depression, even talking of suicide. A short course of psychotherapy helped but she was still faced with withdrawal discomfort, an increasing reliance on alcohol and continued Cabaret Card difficulties. Life was getting tough.

She continued to record for Decca in the late 1940s with arrangers like Sy Oliver and Gordon Jenkins, who maintained the standard of quality, jazz-inflected pop set by the Toots Camarata-arranged sides of the mid-1940s, though Billie's tardy time-keeping meant that she would rarely achieve the four sides per session expected. There was a session with Louis Armstrong in which he appeared to swear in the heat of their ribald banter during 'My Sweet Hunk Of Trash' and once spotted, the record had to be withdrawn.

In mid-1950, Gabler was moved to the Decca subsidiary label Coral, and in the absence of such a staunch (and tolerant) believer at the record company and with conspicuously less support on the airwaves for her latest sides, Billie was dropped. 'Just say the top echelon didn't want to risk it,' said Gabler. 'She was getting a lot of notoriety…They figured there would be problems.'

Gabler is justly satisfied of his achievements with Billie Holiday. 'I'm very proud that I recorded Billie and got her at the peak of her vocal abilities. You can hear the warmth and fullness of her voice in those recordings.' Though these days, the Decca sides are held in affectionate regard by many observers as quality period pop music, it was not always so. Though some commentators like *Metronome* were encouraging about the results, other listeners were disappointed at the lack of jazz content in the recordings ('I caught hell on *Down Beat*,' remembered Gabler) and some – for whom the presence of 'jazz' remains more important that the sympathetic presentation of a song worth singing – remain sceptical. However, for many listeners, Billie's Decca sides are the most accessible and likeable music she ever made.

In August 1950, there was a disastrous tour with West Coast trumpeter Gerald Wilson that left Billie and the band stranded without any money. She got funds wired through by Levy but reneged on a promise to send for the band and left the Musician's Union to sort out the messy business. However, one positive thing that occurred was that she finally left John Levy after a booking in Washington DC, again temporarily reuniting with husband Jimmy Monroe.

Through 1950–51, there were further problems: she missed shows, her chauffeur was arrested in possession of heroin and her attorney from the 1949 trial had her car impounded in lieu of his unpaid bill. But there was also work in San Francisco, Detroit, Philadelphia and a season at Chicago's Hi-Note Club with Miles Davis. She even made four creditable sides for Aladdin Records, a West Coast R&B label, and even found a certain romantic stability in the shape of 'a tall, brown-skinned, serious-minded fellow' she had known since the 1930s named Louis McKay.

Seeking him out in Detroit where he had a job in a car plant, he refused her plea to help and accompany her on the road until she was 'ready to kick her drug habit', as he said. Reports from her October 1951 engagement in Boston confirmed that here was a revitalised Lady Day displaying a 'new sense of responsibility', as *Down Beat* observed. She even seemed to be enjoying her singing again, offering to perform extra sets for radio broadcast.

Another break came in the form of Norman Granz. He had met Billie in 1942 in Hollywood when she was appearing at the Trouville club and he was a college student and a film cutter at MGM Studios. Like Gabler in New York, he was also promoting jam sessions and began recording musicians in 1942, starting with a Nat Cole–Lester Young session. He promoted and recorded a Nat Cole–Les Paul–Illinois Jacquet concert at the Philharmonic Auditorium, Los Angeles, in 1944 – all swinging tempos and extended solos – and thus the 'Jazz At The Philharmonic' formula was born. The issued records and touring jam-session-in-a-concert-hall shows were an enormous success.

Granz was fan enough to have featured Billie in his 'Jazz At The Philharmonic' concerts when he could, but he felt her 1940s Decca recordings had muted that 'spontaneous feel' he had loved so about her work with Teddy Wilson in the 1930s. Between 1952 and 1957, he supervised many sessions that attempted to duplicate the spirit of those earlier recordings, gathering players such as Granz favourite pianist Oscar Peterson, guitarist Barney Kessel and trumpeter Charlie Shavers, alongside old pals of Billie's like Ben Webster, Harry 'Sweets' Edison and Buck Clayton.

Keen to get her away from the set-in-stone, unlucky-in-life repertoire of her live appearances into the unexplored (by her) corners of the American Songbook, Granz encouraged Billie to learn new tunes. 'Norman brought her some more difficult songs to sing...that were quite different from what she would have chosen,' remembered Barney Kessel. 'They were beyond her usual range of expression, songs whose nuances she would have to make some effort to master. Sometimes she felt like making the effort, and sometimes she didn't. When she didn't, in a gentle way she'd kind of – well, "quarrel" is not the word and "argue" isn't the word either – let's say "discuss" it with a different, definite point of view. Sometimes Norman would persist and sometimes he would back off. But I think most of the time he got his way because she felt that, when the effort was made, she was very happy with the results.'

The sessions were determinedly spontaneous, which Billie loved. 'We never knew which tunes we were going to record until we got to the studio,' remembered Oscar Peterson. 'Norman didn't bring any music to the studio. His idea was to help her figure out what she'd like to do. They'd be laughing and talking in the corner by the spare piano. Then she'd walk over, say "I used to do this," and begin singing.' Oscar sometimes was not sure of the tune 'but the way she sang it, we could hear the key and just begin playing behind her. It would automatically become a run-through and as soon as it was over, she'd go to the mike and say "All right, let's try one now." I'd say, "Wait a minute, Billie –", but she was off and running. I didn't always have time to work out a written introduction for her, but she didn't care. She'd just say, "Play those little things you play, and I'll come in."'

Inevitably, given her drinking, smoking and drug-taking, there was a deterioration of the quality of her singing voice. It was a gradual decline but not a consistent one. Some nights she would be reported as having little more than an Armstrong-esque guttural growl (as in 1951), while elsewhere sounding in 'wonderful form' (in 1953).

The experience of the expressive singing voice is a very subjective one. Where one listener may only hear insecure pitching, inflexible timbre and limited range (John S Wilson in *The New York Times* said: 'depending largely on mannerisms to carry her through...she seemed reduced to a ragged, wavering ghost of the inspired singer she once was, straining for the remembered effects she can no longer achieve') another may hear a moving performance of a lyric that resonates with the subtext of a life lived to the full. Miles Davis was one of them: 'I'd rather hear her now,' he said in the 1950s, 'she's become much more mature...and she still has control, probably more now than then.'

And as Billie asserted herself in *Lady Sings The Blues*, 'Anybody who knows anything about singing says I'm for sure singing better than I ever have in my life...Listen and trust your own ears. For God's sake, don't listen to those tired old columnists who are still writing about the good old days twenty years ago.'

Still suffering from the denial of a Cabaret Card, Billie was able to perform at prestigious venues like the Apollo and

Carnegie Hall but still had to look outside of New York for club work. Despite a painful tooth abscess in autumn 1953, her mood was optimistic enough to agree to feature in a TV programme called *Comeback* in which she frankly discussed her addiction and incarceration. Featuring contributions from Count Basie, Leonard Feather and Artie Shaw, the programme cemented the ever-present relationship between Billie's art and the legend of her struggle with life. It was a relationship she would continue to exploit for the rest of her career.

Early 1954 saw Billie fulfil a long-held ambition to tour Europe and although the arduous trip contributed to a lacklustre opening show in Stockholm, the remainder of the visit, including a handful of dates in Britain, were received with great affection and acclaim. Billie met up with singer Annie Ross in Paris, where they went on a drinking and shoplifting expedition. 'It was just that she really got a big kick out of lifting something from a very high class establishment,' remembered Ross.

Billie was clearly cheered by the rapturous reception given to her by fans and press alike, but the highlight of the European experience was the February concert in front of 6,000 people at the Royal Albert Hall, London, with the Jack Parnell Band. Parnell found her 'friendly, down to earth, but with tremendous swings and changes of moods'. The fact that her pianist at the time, Carl Drinkard, was Billie's occasional heroin buddy did not help things. 'Her and her pianist got so out of it we found it very difficult to do what we had rehearsed,' remembered Parnell, 'but terrific, there's no doubt about that'. Billie even went on to sing an after-hours set at Soho club The Flamingo, full of musicians who had missed the Albert Hall concert.

Back in the USA, a highlight of 1954 was the first Newport Jazz Festival in July, which found Billie reunited with a familiar-sounding line-up including Teddy Wilson, Buck Clayton and trombonist Vic Dickenson, all veterans of Billie's classic Columbia sides. Later they were joined by Lester Young in a poignant moment given a 'Feud Is Over' spin by *Down Beat*. Lester and Billie had apparently fallen out in the early 1950s over his disapproval of her heroin habit but both were conspicuously happy to be pals again.

Billie benefited from the mid-1950s boom in large-scale jazz concerts and appeared at many of them, but it still irked her that she was denied the chance to sing in New York clubs, for several reasons. One, her art was essentially an intimate one and open-air festivals, however lucrative and gratifying in terms of acclaim, could never duplicate the connection between performer and audience that can occur in a club. Two, it was the principle of the thing; she told UK reporters she knew 'some kids been in trouble two or three times are still working. So why pick on me?' Three, it was a valuable source of income and career leverage that was simply denied her.

September 1954 saw her back at Carnegie Hall on 'an off night' according to *Down Beat,* who never shrunk from telling it how they saw it. However, the magazine had honoured her in Los Angeles by devising a special award of 'one of the great all-time vocalists in jazz'. Billie had been disappointed in never winning one of their Best Singer polls and this award sent her the message that the jazz commentators cared about her and rated her highly, for which she was grateful.

However, Billie's inconsistent moods and unpredictable personal appearances continued to alienate some. Oscar Peterson tells a significant story of a 1954 concert at Carnegie Hall where, after a successful first set, someone had 'got to her' in the interval. 'I took one look at her and she was like the sphinx, like a graven image,' he remembered. 'I laid down the intro to "I Only Have Eyes For You". She missed the point where she was supposed to come in...I made a fast U-turn and went back, playing a more definitive intro, figuring she didn't hear the first one. She went right past that one too. You could hear odd little whispers in the audience. God it was horrible.'

Billie eventually started singing 'but she never went into tempo,' remembered Peterson. 'We tried to find the time for her, but we couldn't lock her in, couldn't bring her back...It didn't last long. Norman came out and led her offstage.'

Backstage, Billie had no doubt where the blame lay. 'Billie was sitting there and said: "There's Oscar Peterson. That so-and-so screwed up my music."... She knew she had goofed up and there wasn't any way to recoup it, except to try and shift the blame.' It was the last time Peterson played for Billie Holiday.

Maely Bartholemew had been Billie's informal assistant for several years and had recently married *New York Post* reporter William Dufty. When there was talk of a biography, which intensified in the light of the success of Louis Armstrong's and Ethel Waters' books, Dufty was in place to do it. With a working title of *Bitter Crop* (from a line in 'Strange Fruit'), he set about fashioning a compelling, seamy tale told in hard-bitten, first-person street prose, based on Billie's unreliable reminiscences and his own imagination.

There seems little doubt that Louis McKay had been some kind of stabilising influence on Billie. Yes, he beat her, bought property with her money in his name (which never appeared as part of Billie's estate when she died) but given his declared hard-line disapproval of her heroin habit, there had appeared to be a reduction at least in Billie's drug intake. So, it was a surprising setback in February 1956 when she and McKay were arrested for possession and use of drugs in a Philadelphia hotel room. Heroin and cocaine were discovered and both Billie and McKay were found to be under the influence of narcotics. McKay claimed later that they had been harassed and set up, but Billie checked into a hospital to detoxify with substitute drugs. The result was that she began drinking up to two bottles of spirits a day.

The publication in August 1956 of the 'autobiography' – now called *Lady Sings The Blues* – was accompanied by a newly recorded album of the same name featuring Billie-related tunes. Though it was said that Billie Holiday never even read the book, she did not shy from promoting an association with it, even participating in a November 1956 Carnegie Hall concert in which excerpts of the book were read aloud by *New York Times* journalist Gilbert Millstein. He remembers Billie arriving at Carnegie Hall's rehearsal rooms with Louis McKay and Joe Glaser. 'She could never have gotten to the rehearsal hall, someone had to bring her there because she was half gone…Her legs were swollen, she was almost incoherent, she had no more idea of what to sing than I did.'

And yet, miraculously, the evening was a massive success. 'It was the most haphazard [thing] with which I've ever been associated in my life,' remembered Millstein, 'and yet it came off as though it had been machine tooled'. Millstein later wrote of a transformation as show time arrived. 'The lights went down, the musicians began to play and the narration began. Miss Holiday stepped from between the curtains, into the white spotlight awaiting her, wearing a white evening gown and white gardenias in her black hair. She was erect and beautiful; poised and smiling. And when the first section of the narration was ended, she sang – with strength undiminished – with all the art that was hers.'

The concert established the 'Billie Holiday – Survivor' industry with clearer focus than ever before. The legends of the book added to the ubiquitous personality-defining Holiday repertoire ('Don't Explain', 'My Man', 'I Cried For You', 'T'ain't Nobody's Business If I Do') and created once and for all the big-hearted-victim-of-life image that endures to this day. The recording that was released shows Millstein did not exaggerate the quality of Billie's performance.

The February 1956 narcotics charge still hung over her, however, and in order to avoid having to testify against each other, Billie and Louis McKay were married in March 1957. By June, discovering that Billie was back on drugs and probably entertaining sexual attentions from her lawyer Earle Zaidins, McKay left her in New York and settled on the West Coast. Billie appeared a month later at the Newport Jazz Festival which was recorded and released (along with an Ella Fitzgerald set) as Billie's final outing on Verve. Granz had clearly had enough documenting a palpably diminishing and self-destructive talent and did not renew Billie's contract. 'I think we did all we could together,' he reflected later.

In December 1957, Billie took part in a now legendary telecast called *The Sound Of Jazz*, in which she sang her blues 'Fine and Mellow', accompanied by several horn players from her life each taking a chorus in a performance that lasts over eight minutes. It is a remarkable piece of film with Billie looking and sounding happy and healthy, surrounded by these men who take turns to parade their musical wares under the appreciative gaze of the Queen of Song. 'I couldn't believe how "sexy" Billie Holiday was until I saw the TV stuff on her,' commented jazz singer Mark Murphy. 'She had such an overwhelming sexuality, I was quite, you know, shocked. She didn't have to do anything, it was just "there".' There is something undeniably sensual and tender about Billie's facial expressions as she savours the contributions of Ben Webster, Coleman Hawkins and Roy Eldridge, but she saves her big nod of affectionate appreciation for the moving solo by the desperately ill Lester Young.

By late 1957, Billie had signed back with Columbia after fifteen years and on hearing one of his moody easy listening albums, *Ellis In Wonderland*, was determined to make an album with arranger Ray Ellis. Scheduled to begin in October ('she blew about twenty-five appointments,' remembered Ellis), the sessions, featuring a full string orchestra, choir and harpist, eventually began in February 1958. Ellis was shocked by the state of her voice and Billie, drunk and insecure, took out her problems on Ellis. 'I cut two songs out and I finally realised that this bitch doesn't know the song and she's putting *me* down because *she* doesn't know it.' Ellis persuaded her to take a break ('I had to treat her like a school kid') and learn the material, particularly some verses she didn't know, with pianist Mal Waldron. 'She gave me a lot of dirty looks,' remembered Ellis, 'but she did learn the verses'.

Recorded over three tortuous days, by the time *Lady In Satin* was finished, Ellis was disenchanted, to say the least ('I was completely bugged, frustrated, disgusted, finished with it') and he couldn't even face mixing the album. Producer Irving Townsend sent over a test pressing several months later and Ellis remembers, 'It hit me finally. It didn't matter whether she sang the right note or the wrong note, because she sang 25,000 wrong notes on that one. She poured her heart out.'

A vividly coloured cover, sumptuous strings and a cracked voice at the centre that seems the vocal embodiment of a breaking spirit, it is some listeners' favourite record – for others it is an all-time downer. 'Every time I listen to it I get depressed,' confessed Ellis. It's not surprising that a purveyor of pristine gloop like Ellis should find the record hard to take, nor that Billie was immensely proud of it. These are typically disparate reactions to what remains the single most controversial album in Billie Holiday's catalogue. Many people despise the record, finding the lush strings and choir cushioning Lady's barely functioning, ravaged instrument on an attractive selection of stylish compositions too incongruous an experience to take.

Billie's alcoholism and drug habit were by now taking their dreadful toll on her health. The hearing for the February 1956 narcotics rap came up in March 1958 and though she escaped jail (receiving twelve months' probation), physically she was getting weaker, and artistically she was doing little more than going through the motions. Inevitably, her personal appearances were more erratic than ever. She had to be helped onto the stage and held upright to perform at the Monterey Jazz Festival in October 1958 and was booed on a brief European tour in November. Neither the audience or the critics spared her; *Down Beat* described a performance of that period as 'a sing-along routine which she adheres to with almost pathetic tenacity'.

However, an appearance in September 1958 at Leonard Feather's 'Seven Ages Of Jazz' festival displayed a heartier Holiday and, amazingly, a performance for a February 1959 TV show recorded in London displayed considerable fortitude. Billie was thin and her singing measured and careful, but there is a dramatic focus and wealth of experience in her readings of 'Porgy' and 'Strange Fruit' as she, once more, makes the most of what little she had left.

Almost inevitably, there were further blows. An incident in which she was threatened with prison by the US Customs Service for violating the Narcotics Control Acts (she failed to register before leaving and upon returning to the country) was eventually settled, but not before Billie suffered much anxiety. Then, in March 1959, Lester Young died and Billie, distraught with grief and anger at not being allowed to sing at his funeral, was filled with her own sense of mortality. 'I'll be the next to go,' she told friend and writer Leonard Feather.

Yet in April at the Storyville, Boston, and in May at the Flamingo in Massachusetts Billie delivered spirited shows, with her pianist Mal Waldron observing, 'she was weak but she always sang well.' But most people who had known her before and saw her in this period were shocked at her weight loss, with Leonard Feather barely recognising the disorientated, dribbling old woman backstage at the Jazz At The Phoenix show as his old friend Billie. Feather and Joe Glaser tried to persuade Billie into hospital but she was afraid and refused. She finally collapsed on 30 May.

A farcical and tragic air surrounded her admittance to hospital. She was taken by ambulance to Knickerbocker Hospital, New York, and left unattended before being diagnosed as an alcohol- and drug-related case and therefore not eligible for admission at a private hospital unless in a critical condition. Transferred to the Metropolitan, she again remained unattended until her doctor, who had been chasing her from hospital to hospital, arrived and insisted on attention for his patient.

Billie was placed under an oxygen tent and was eventually diagnosed as suffering from a liver ailment complicated by cardiac failure. While she slowly recovered, gaining weight and strength, her attorney Zaidins continued to operate on her behalf – but not, perhaps, in her best interest – signing her to a movie and a new agent, even though Joe Glaser had announced he was underwriting all medical bills.

Eleven days after Billie was admitted to hospital, a nurse found some cocaine and the police arrested Billie, confiscated her belongings and sealed off her room with a police guard. Legal wrangling held off the threat of imminent incarceration and the following month saw Billie begin to recover sufficiently to begin dictating more of her autobiography to William Dufty. She suffered a relapse and received last rites on 15 July, rallied the next day, but died in the early hours of 17 July 1959, aged forty-four.

When her estate was assessed, it hardly amounted to $1,500. All future earnings in her name went to the estranged but not divorced Louis McKay. There was a mass on 21 July at St Paul's Roman Catholic Church on Columbus Circle attended by 3,000 people, including bassist Milt Hinton who remembered 'such a quietness over these musicians. Just dead quiet and sadness'.

One of the temptations in the telling of the Billie Holiday story is to attempt to spot the villain. If one is so inclined, one is spoilt for choice. Standing culpable of at least some share of responsibility for this pitiful tale – to a greater or lesser extent according to interpretation – are the following: Sadie, the neglectful mother, the hopeless role-model; Clarence, the absent, vain father; Wilbert Rich (Mr Dick), the rapist; Florence Williams, the opportunistic madam; Ed Fox, the crazy manager of Chicago's Grand Terrace (representing all insensitive employers); the redneck who called her the 'nigger wench' (representing all ignorant racists); the manager of New York's Lincoln Hotel who asked her to use the freight elevators (representing all informed racism); the unidentified friend who first introduced her to heroin; Jimmy Monroe, Joe Guy, John Levy, Louis McKay, long-term husbands/lovers who beat her, stole her money and were not able to or had no interest in helping her resist drugs; Joe Glaser, the effective if brutal booking agent of elusive motivation; Earle Warren Zaidins, the incompetent lawyer pursuing blatant self-interest; the New York Police Department and the Federal Bureau Of Narcotics.

And yet tough upbringing and routine racism aside (which after all, many millions of people endure without reaching Billie's highs or suffering her lows), it is unlikely Billie would apportion blame for her fortunes to anyone but herself. At the risk of once more blurring the distinction between her life and her art – just as she would have had us do – when we hear her sing the opening from ''Tain't Nobody's Business If I Do' ('There ain't nothin' I ever do/Or nothin' I ever say/That folks don't criticise me/But I'm going to do just as I want anyway') it is hard not to sense in those lines the essence of how she chose to live. Her destructive habits may have started out as ways to stave off pain and get some fun out of life, but they became almost symbols of defiance and independence in the straight, white world. 'If I ever have a notion/To jump into the ocean/It ain't nobody's business if I do.'

TWO

THE MUSIC

The recorded musical career of Billie Holiday can be handily identified as having three phases: the John Hammond–Bernie Hanighen–Morty Palitz productions of the Columbia period 1933–1942, the Milt Gabler productions for Commodore and Decca 1939–1950 and the Norman Granz productions for Clef and Verve 1952–1957. The two Ray Ellis albums of 1958 and 1959 can be regarded as a coda.

Pre-Verve (and soon, undoubtedly, post-Verve) Billie Holiday recordings have been subject to a slew of budget releases – in other words, those that repackage 'public domain' recordings (those over fifty years old) at minimal cost – and they are often quite temptingly cheap if one is merely curious to hear what all the fuss is about. However, the variable quality in both packaging and sound production means that the listener may well be short-changed in one way or another. For sensibly annotated, carefully compiled issues, it is probably best to head for the official releases under the Columbia/Commodore/Decca/Verve banners, and it is these CDs that we shall turn to in discussion of Billie's musical career.

Billie's Brunswick/Vocalian/Columbia/Okeh recordings were more or less definitively compiled (eccentric sleeve notes notwithstanding) into nine volumes entitled *The Quintessential Billie Holiday* in the Columbia Jazz Masterpieces series released in 1987–91. Still available in the US (but only on import in the UK), they remain the authoritative chronological guide to Billie's classic sides of the 1930s and early 1940s, all 153 of them.

THE COLUMBIA YEARS 1933–1942

The Quintessential Billie Holiday Volume 1 1933–1935

(CK 40646)

Your Mother's Son-In-Law/Riffin'The Scotch/I Wished On The Moon/What A Little Moonlight Can Do/Miss Brown To You/A Sunbonnet Blue/What A Night,What A Moon,What A Girl/I'm Painting The Town Red/It's Too Hot For Words/ Twenty-Four Hours A Day/Yankee Doodle Never Went To Town/Eeny Meeny Miney Mo/If You Were Mine/These 'N'That 'N'Those/You Let Me Down/ Spreadin' Rhythm Around

Billie Holiday's recording career begins with the two cuts made under Benny Goodman's name in November and December 1933, a pair of lumpy rhythm novelties featuring Goodman's dancing clarinet and Jack Teagarden's plangent trombone sandwiching an eager vocal from nervous, nineteen-year-old Billie Holiday. Though Billie was later to laugh at the high, happy sound she made on 'Your Mother's Son-in-law' and 'Riffin' The Scotch' ('it sounds like I'm doing comedy'), these performances already show that like Louis Armstrong, this teenager's vocal phrasing has an independence that will not be bound by the clear 4/4 groundbeat as laid down by the band. Modest but palpable dragging and pushing and a precocious little trill ('right into the fi-i-re') all betray a talent virtually in place. 'You're not going to let these people think you're a square, are you?' encouraged pianist Buck Washington to banish Billie's nerves. That was the last thing she was going to do.

July 1935 saw the first Hammond-produced Teddy Wilson session that set the tone for the majestic Wilson–Holiday sides of the period. Informal arrangements featuring plenty of Wilson's immaculate pianistic commentary (his 'pearly' arpeggios, as Gunther Schuller has it) and the best jazz musicians – in this case including Goodman (clarinet), Roy Eldridge (trumpet) and Ben Webster (tenor saxophone) – surrounding a single chorus vocal by this curiously-voiced young lady.

'I Wished On The Moon' is pitched slightly too low for Billie (the 'day' of 'On April day', glissandos awkwardly down to an undetermined pitch) but she recasts the final line into her open-throated sweet spot, brilliantly setting the dynamic for the band's thrilling out chorus. On 'What A Little Moonlight Can Do' Billie is rhythmically confident but unhurried, despite the freewheeling tempo. The sound she makes – from the guttural growl of 'words I love you' to the moonshine clarity of 'can't resist him' – is uniquely appealing. It is a measure of her confidence that she feels free enough to utter asides of approval and encouragement during Wilson's solo on

'Miss Brown To You'. The final cut, a sentimental Tin Pan Alley shocker called 'A Sunbonnet Blue (And A Little Straw Hat)' would not be the last sow's ear Billie and her musicians would gamely attempt to fashion into a silk purse. Although complaints about the B-list quality of some of the songs Billie was required to sing have often been overstated – many of these minor compositions have their own considerable charm - it's hard to warm to this one.

The obvious success of that first session did not stop Wilson trying to formalise the arrangements with unison riffs and organised bridging passages for the follow-up session of July 1935. Though Wilson retrospectively admitted to being disappointed with the results, the ensembles swing, the soloists sparkle and Billie sings delightfully, negotiating the verbose, suggestive 'It's Too Hot For Words' with élan.

Woofy-toned saxophonist Chu Berry replaced Webster and Bennie Morton contributed witty trombone to the October 1935 session, which reverted to casual but absorbing head arrangements. Billie approaches the wordy rhythmic requirements of 'Twenty-Four Hours A Day', 'Yankee Doodle Never Went To Town' and 'Eeny Meeny Miney Mo' with archetypal, dawdling elegance and Eldridge is on particularly exciting form on 'Eeny'. 'These 'N' That 'N' Those' from the December 1935 session is the sort of ingenious list song that reeks of contrivance but somehow wins your heart by its very silliness and eagerness to please: 'These are moments rare/And that's a comfy chair/And these are lips that should be kissed/How can we resist these 'n' that 'n' those.' Billie indulges in some melodramatic dying notes ('Those two arms have room to spa-a-are') but somehow convinces us that this is a song worth singing.

'You Let Me Down', by contrast, is a Harry Warren–Al Dubin (of 42nd Street fame) masterpiece that so suits Billie's later minor key, unlucky-in-life persona, it's surprising she never returned to it. 'You Let Me Down' was also significant in that it was the first time Billie's vocal 'led' the recording, an indicator of things to come.

The Quintessential Billie Holiday Volume 2 1936

(CK 40790)

Life Begins When You're In Love/It's Like Reaching For The Moon/These Foolish Things/I Cried For You/Guess Who/Did I Remember?/No Regrets/Summertime/Billie's Blues/A Fine Romance/I Can't Pretend/One, Two, Button Your Shoe/Let's Call A Heart A Heart/Easy To Love/With Thee I Swing/The Way You Look Tonight

The amiable 'Life Begins When You're In Love' was the only side Billie sang on during the January 1936 session but the June 1936 session was productive and rich. Hammond would book musicians from whatever band was in town and in this case, it must have been Ellington's, with Harry Carney (baritone and clarinet) and Johnny Hodges (alto) thickening out Wilson's modest orchestra beautifully. 'It's Like Reaching For The Moon' and 'These Foolish Things' see Billie unusually experimenting with vibrato and further indulging in fluttering fall-offs at the end of notes partly as a cover-up ('Things' is clearly not the right key for her), partly as a not altogether well-judged and thankfully rare attempt to force emotion from the music. Still, she makes light work of Freed and Lane's throwaway 'Sweet Sue' variation, 'Guess Who'.

In July 1936, not two weeks later, Billie was under the guiding hand of lover, producer and marijuana pal Bernie Hanighen, leading her own session, producing records to be issued as by Billie Holiday And Her Orchestra for the first time. Naturally, Billie's vocal leads the arrangement but also, for the first time for her on record, it reprises at the end, often from the bridge to the close. Featuring Artie Shaw (clarinet), Bunny Berigan (trumpet) and Joe Bushkin (piano), the cuts are very similar in spirit to the Wilson-led sides (without the glittering cascades of piano notes) and Billie leads with confidence and purpose. 'Did I Remember' is an enchanting swinger, the long, high melody delivered by Billie with clarion-call lucidity, 'No Regrets' has a magnetic sassiness (especially when compared to contemporary melancholy versions of the song), 'Summertime' – not yet nine months old – is given an atmospheric treatment by the band with Billie re-shaping the melody (partly to suit her range) into a memorable bluesy paraphrase.

Though Billie's singing was infused with blues feeling and characteristics, she is often mistakenly referred to as a blues singer when in fact she recorded only a few blues tunes. The first occasion was at this July 1936 session where the legend goes that nobody liked the fourth tune (it would be intriguing to know which song it was) and Hanighen encouraged Billie to invent a blues then and there. 'Billie's Blues' was her first copyright and far from being just a Bessie Smith-esque moaning wail, it's a good early example of her rigorously melodic approach to blues material. Interestingly, this was an all-white band (apart from Billie and drummer Cozy Cole) and while opinions are divided as to how well they do with this most Afro-American of idioms, there's no mistaking the convincing, startling work of the vocalist.

Two months later, in September 1936, Billie led another of her own sessions, retaining Berigan but adding Irving Fazola (clarinet) and Clyde Hart (piano). She sneers through Kern and Fields' sarcastic love song 'A Fine Romance' in a good example of the kind of part-pragmatic, part-aesthetic re-structuring of a rangy melody into a neat summary of the important points. It was this kind of re-composing that inspired one song-writer to remark, 'that's a nice job, but it isn't my tune.' 'I Can't Pretend' is a rather lugubrious obscurity featuring a hearty Billie vocal and some odd percussion effects from a restless-sounding Cole while 'One, Two, Button Your Shoe' leads off with some drummer and singer banter ('Get on back to them drums, I'll start this band!'). Both 'Shoe' and 'Let's Call A Heart A Heart' were throwaways from a Bing Crosby movie of that year, but the band are fine and Billie 'commits' to the songs, producing music of enduring charm.

Billie was back with Wilson and a heap of Goodman men in October 1936 doing a Porter ('Easy To Love' audaciously ironed out to suit, though not entirely), a Kern ('The Way You Look Tonight', where this group's carefree attitude perhaps spills over into carelessness – 'they butcher it' screams The Quintessential Billie Holiday compiler Michael Brooks) and a knocked-off Old-English rhythm novelty, 'With Thee I Swing'. As listenable as ever, though one may be allowed to detect a temporary dip in standards.

The Quintessential Billie Holiday Volume 3
1936–1937

(CK44048)

Who Loves You?/Pennies From Heaven/That's Life I Guess/I Can't Give You Anything But Love (Baby)/One Never Knows – Does One?/I've Got My Love To Keep Me Warm/If My Heart Could Only Talk/Please Keep Me In Your Dreams/He Ain't Got Rhythm/This Year's Kisses/Why Was I Born/I Must Have That Man/The Mood That I'm In/You Showed Me The Way/Sentimental And Melancholy/My Last Affair

A quick one-cut session with Wilson in October 1936 produced 'Who Loves You?', a typically engaged performance of second division material, while November 1936 saw Billie back with Wilson, Goodman and Webster along with Jonah Jones (trumpet) for a fine session, turning out an exemplary reading of 'Pennies From Heaven' (with pungent, horn-like choices of notes from Billie), 'That's Life I Guess' (a resigned piece suited to Billie's world-weary delivery, it could have been written for her, but wasn't) and 'I Can't Give You Anything But Love' (a stunning, Armstrong-esque recasting of the 1928 warhorse).

12 January 1937 saw Teddy Wilson as hired hand for a Billie Holiday-led session for the first time, a sure sign that things were happening around the singer. Perhaps Hanighen (or Hammond) sensed something lacking in the previous Wilson-free Holiday sessions and the poised pianist certainly injects a certain characteristic sparkle back into the music. Webster and Jones's robust contributions and Billie's touching delivery (especially of 'One Never Knows – Does One' and 'Please Keep Me In Your Dreams') mark the session as a superior Holiday-led one of the period.

However, it was the session under Wilson's name only two weeks later on 25 January 1937 that was the more significant event. Hammond, as usual, cast around town for suitable musicians and was currently closely involved with the Count Basie Orchestra's shaky New York debut. Despite his disappointment, he had enough faith in the instrumental capabilities of Basie-ites Lester Young (tenor sax), Buck Clayton (trumpet), Walter Page (bass), and Jo Jones (drums) to team them with Goodman, Wilson and Holiday. He also invited an unknown guitarist named Freddie Green who, within days of the session, was invited to join Basie – to complete what was later routinely referred to as the world's greatest rhythm section – and stayed until the mid-1980s.

As far as Billie Holiday's music was concerned, it had never quite been blessed with musicians of such empathy and discretion before. There's a hip lightness instantly recognisable from the understated, Goodman-led opening chorus of Irving Berlin's amusing novelty 'He Ain't Got Rhythm' to which Billie immediately responds by delivering a perfectly measured vocal. Lester takes the cue, presenting eighteen bars (the song has a strange form) of his particular, soft-edged brand of swinging perfection, Buck picks out some pristine arpeggios and the others creep in for a modest free-for-all to close. Taken individually, the elements of this performance (and others like it) are not so remarkable, but when put

together in an organic whole, they create a wonder.
Another Berlin tune, 'This Year's Kisses', opens with Lester
breathing the twenty-eight bar theme (another strange
form) into our ears with alluring tenderness. This time
Billie takes the cue, producing a deliciously warm vocal,
followed by Wilson and Clayton, both treading daintily.
'Why Was I Born' spotlights Clayton's trim muted trumpet to which Billie responds by underplaying the melodramatic despair in the lyric with attractive restraint.

The acknowledged highlight of an historic session is 'I
Must Have That Man'. It leads with a poised and
confident Billie, not shying from getting into the cracks of
Jimmy McHugh's cramped melodic shapes while still
finding time to decorate the phrases with subtle decorative gestures; it is a vocal that represents no less than
a jazz singer coming of age. Lester follows with a half-
chorus of sly, slow-eyed sensitivity and Goodman
responds to the mood with great musical grace. Billie
biographer Donald Clarke suggests without embarrass-
ment: 'Music in Heaven is like this'.

If a Wilson-led date of 18 February 1937 didn't quite
have the same refinement as 25 January, it certainly
had vigour. Featuring Henry 'Red' Allen on trumpet, who
was even more assertive and fiery than Roy Eldridge (if
not everyone's idea of suitable accompaniment for Lady
Day), Billie responds magnificently by delivering four
clean, positive vocals of great musical control on 'The
Mood That I'm In', Ella Fitzgerald's 'You Show Me The
Way', Johnny Mercer's 'Sentimental And Melancholy' and
'This Is My Last Affair'. It may be that the preceding session has overshadowed the fine work on this one, but
Allen's spirited contributions and Billie's excellent singing
mark it as being first class.

The Quintessential Billie Holiday Volume 4 1937

(CK 44252)

Carelessly/How Could You?/Moanin' Low/Where Is
The Sun?/Let's Call The Whole Thing Off/They Can't
Take That Away From Me/I Don't Know If I'm
Coming Or Going/Sun Showers/Yours And Mine/I'll
Get By/Mean To Me/Foolin' Myself/Easy Living/I'll
Never Be The Same/Me, Myself And I/A Sailboat In
The Moonlight

*By March 1937 Billie had been offered the female
singing job with Basie. Just before her debut, a couple of
recording sessions were squeezed in. John Hammond
was not apparently enamoured of the Ellington band
but clearly thought enough of Cootie Williams (trumpet)
to hire him and was pleased enough with Johnny
Hodges (alto saxophone) and Harry Carney (clarinet,
baritone) to rehire them for a Wilson-led date on 31
March. 'Carelessly' is handled respectfully and affectingly, 'How Could You' bounces along with the effortless,
carefree quality that Billie had shown was such a natural part of her since 'Your Mother's Son In Law'. 'Moanin'
Low' shows that even when the material invites a tragic
air (she loves her man, even though he's mean), Billie
plays out the role of browbeaten, faithful partner with
believable dignity; she does indeed sound like the 'kind
of woman' that 'kind of a man needs'. It is a theme she
would return to.*

*The following day, 1 April 1937, Billie led her own
session featuring Wilson along with Joe Thomas (tenor)
and Eddie Tompkins (trumpet), both members of
the Jimmie Lunceford Orchestra. 'Where Is The Sun' is a*

lovely reading of an obscure song, Billie's performance of which is relatively rare; the below-par audio quality meant that the song was often omitted from earlier collections of the period. Billie had been tempted to cover songs from recent Fred Astaire films before ('A Fine Romance', 'The Way You Look Tonight') and here she tries two Gershwins from the film Carefree, *'Let's Call The Whole Thing Off' and 'They Can't Take That Away From Me'. The former is relatively unconvincing – Billie struggles to make the repetitive wordplay swing and indulges in several dying butterfly 'ohh's in the bridge – but the latter's easy lope and spacious melody fits Billie like a glove. 'I Don't Know If I'm Coming Or Going' is a little known Cotton Club delight with an intriguing climbing melody and a triple rhyme which Billie times to perfection.*

Billie Holiday never officially recorded with the full Basie band (they were contracted to separate companies) and if the few extant air checks are anything to go by (look for the tell-tale coupling of 'Swing Brother Swing' and 'They Can't Take That Away From Me' on the track-list of a public domain CD), it's very much our loss. Billie sounds stimulated by the Basie orchestra's hard driving swing and it is clear that the band and singer could have gone on to make some great music. However, her experience with Basie helped Billie's singing generally and Basie-ites continued to appear on Wilson's and her own small group recordings.

Buck Clayton and Lester Young joined Johnny Hodges on the Wilson-led session of May 1937 and among the tunes examined was Turk and Ahlert's 'I'll Get By', which is among the most famous of Billie's early recordings. Following Hodges's characteristically glissandi-ordained but robustly swinging reading of the melody, Billie re-shapes the tune to fit almost entirely on one repeated, daringly timed note, a high A (the third note in the key of F major). The effect is one of a freely tolling bell of sur-vival, unpredictable but unassailable; she will indeed get by. The same composers were responsible for 'Mean To Me', this time led by sixteen exquisite bars of Lester Young and capped by a deliciously re-framed melody à la Holiday. Here we can hear the dazzling range of her rhythmic and melodic manipulations in all its happy, unselfconscious splendour. 'Mean To Me' ranks in the Top Ten of all Billie's performances.

A pair of sessions in June 1937 imported Basie's rhythm section as a unit to a Wilson-led session on the 1st of the month and a Holiday-led date on the 15th. The Basie men were apparently unsure of Wilson's gen-tlemanly, decorative approach to the music at first (used as they were to the no-nonsense drive of Basie) but tracks like 'Foolin' Myself' convey an irresistibly breezy and relaxed two-beat groove. Lester lovingly caresses the melody, Wilson is his immaculate self in the bridge, Buck Clayton takes it a little further out and Billie stays pretty faithful to the swooping scales of the tune, while all the time sounding like she is making the whole thing up.

One would have thought the dangerous intervallic dips and arpeggios of Robin and Rainger's 'Easy Living' was ripe for Holiday's horizontal paraphrasing technique – especially given the relaxed romance of the lyric – but she negotiates the lovely melody with insouciant ease, producing yet another vocal performance peak. Wilson's typically tidy reading of 'I'll Never Be The Same' follows Billie's heartfelt vocal with Lester providing soothing notes of commentary and comfort *in the phrasing spaces. This is the first clearly audible example (Lester has previously been off mike) of the sensitive musical chemistry between these close friends – their two musical personalities sounding shaped from the same mould – and a clear indication of why Lester was Billie's favourite of all her collaborating musicians.*

On the Billie-led date two weeks later on 15 June 1937, Wilson is replaced by James Sherman (who is given generous solo space to sound like an even more polite Wilson) and Lester is handed most of the obbligato duties on 'Me, Myself And I' – a limp obscurity that would be entirely forgotten had Billie and Lester not recorded it – and the hard-to-swallow Guy Lombardo hit 'A Sailboat In The Moonlight'. Billie by now is a shoulder-shrugging professional who can give any piece of hokum her best, big-hearted shot, which is exactly what she does.

The Quintessential Billie Holiday Volume 5 1937–1938

(CK44423)

Born To Love/Without Your Love/Getting Some Fun Out Of Life/Who Wants Love?/Trav'lin' All Alone/He's Funny That Way/Nice Work If You Can Get It/Things Are Looking Up/My Man/Can't Help Lovin' Dat Man/My First Impression Of You/When You're Smiling/I Can't Believe That You're In Love With Me/If Dreams Come True/Now They Call It Swing/On The Sentimental Side/Back In Your Own Backyard/When A Woman Loves A Man

Completing the 15 June session, 'Born To Love' is one of those unremarkable tunes Billie feels compelled to reposition around the incessant third note of the key, though the performance is distinguished by a splendid Buck Clayton solo and the rare appearance (in a Billie Holiday treatment) of the song's verse. By contrast the equally obscure 'Without Your Love' is a charmer, with Lester shadowing Billie delightfully, sketching his own subtle subtext behind the singer's melodic styling (those thirds again), ever mindful of the main event.

September 1937 saw Billie leading those Basie fellows once more, with Claude Thornhill replacing James Sherman on piano, on a peach of a session. 'Getting Some Fun Out Of Life' (which must be one of the contenders for a Billie Holiday theme song) is delivered in a curiously tender manner, as if the 'fun' in the lyrics is a prescribed salve to the pain of existence rather than some hedonistic manifesto, and it's all the more convincing because of it.

It is tempting to note that the effectiveness of 'Who Wants Love?' – a clunky, symmetrical song from a Joan Crawford movie – is entirely due to Thornhill's daringly modernistic solo entry and the Lester/Billie magic (she putting a brave face on it, he murmuring the vulnerable truth behind her), but there is something sweet in the composition too.

'Trav'lin' All Alone' (another theme song contender) is the song supposed to have got Billie the singing job at Pod and Jerry's when she failed the dance audition. Avoiding self-pity by casting itself as a perky minor vamp, it is worth listening to just to hear Billie drawl 'feet like heavy stone'. She sings the superior standard 'He's Funny That Way' high and sweet, expressing the position

of being the centre of inexplicable adoration with such winning, naive optimism, you'd love to believe it.

A session back with Wilson in November 1937 saw Billie singing Gershwin via Fred Astaire twice more with 'Nice Work If You Can Get It' and 'Things Are Looking Up'. The latter is taken at a much slower tempo than Fred's and its tentativeness (relative to the optimism of the four-leaf clover/happy-as-a-pup lyric) is particularly effective, as if Billie can barely bring herself to believe her good fortune. Billie once named this title as one of her all-time favourite recordings.

There is an intriguing early version of the 1920s French tune and Billie theme song 'My Man' – taken at quite a bounce and featuring a hilariously inappropriate roaring ending from the band – but without the masochistic lyrics and funereal tempo that would still have Billie singing it twenty years later. She expertly cus- tomises 'Can't Help Lovin' Dat Man' by removing the Negro phonetics, floating the tune and entirely redesign- ing songwriter Jerome Kern's 'blue' cadences. Kern would have hated it.

The two sessions in January 1938 – one for Wilson, one for Billie – featured the same Basie sidemen as the historic January 1937 date (minus Goodman, plus Bennie Morton on trombone) and by now the differ- ences between the leaders' sides are academic and the excellence is routine. The contemporary pop material like 'My First Impression Of You' (a charmingly tranquil presentation of an 'overwhelming' first meeting) and 'Now They Call It Swing' (a daft history of jazz featuring a very rare example of Billie scatting on record, all two pre-composed bars of it) do their job fine, as do the Billie-as-just-another-horn jam sessions of 'When You're

Smiling', 'If Dreams Come True' and 'Back In Your Own Back Yard'.

The jewels include 'I Can't Believe That You're In Love With Me' (with an authoritative, plaintive re-composition of the melody), another I'll-love-the beast-through-thick-and-thin song — the touching and pretty 'When A Woman Loves A Man' — and a gorgeous, straight impression of 'On The Sentimental Side', the enchanting Burke and Monaco tune written for Bing Crosby's movie Dr Rhythm. *These cuts are indeed on the sentimental side, but they are conveyed so beautifully, vocally and instrumentally, if the listener has any kind of sentimental side, it'll be tickled.*

The Quintessential Billie Holiday Volume 6 1938

(CK 45449)

You Go To My Head/The Moon Looks Down And Laughs/If I Were You/Forget If You Can/Having Myself A Time/Says My Heart/I Wish I Had You/I'm Gonna Lock My Heart (And Throw Away The Key)/The Very Thought Of You/I Can't Get Started/I've Got A Date With A Dream/You Can't Be Mine (And Someone Else's Too)/Everybody's Laughing/Here It Is Tomorrow Again/Say It With A Kiss/April In My Heart/I'll Never Fail You

The Billie-led session of May 1938 is generally regarded (by jazz commentators) as relatively unimportant, due to the pop material and stately, organised ensembles (arranged by trumpeter Charlie Shavers) providing cloudy chords rather than improvised obbligatos behind

Billie's vocal. But the songs are actually interesting Tin Pan Alley rarities rather than the fluff some would have us believe and, once more, Billie is on top form. If it is pop music, it is pop music of a high order.

Nobody could argue with Coots and Gillespie's masterpiece of romantic intoxication 'You Go To My Head', sprawling form and all, but 'The Moon Looks Down And Laughs' by Kalmer and Ruby (of 'Three Little Words' fame), the gently assertive 'If I Were You' and the charming 'Thanks For The Memory' re-write 'Forget If You Can' have a melodic appeal of their own, given genuine lustre by Billie's marvellously restrained delivery.

She even holds herself in for another getting-some-fun-out-of-life piece – 'Having Myself A Time' by Robin and Rainger – which so perfectly captures what one imagines as the essence of the young Billie Holiday that it is worth quoting at length. 'I'm having myself a time/I mean having what I want/Wanting what I have/Doing what I like/And liking what I do…I never could save a dime…When I hum songs/They're all dumb songs/But I'm certainly in my prime/I mean I'm happy as a bird flying up above/Want a little love and get a little love/And I'm having myself a time'.

'Time' is from the more loosely organised June 1938 session, during which she also breezes through an early Frank Loesser, 'Says My Heart', the Fats Waller-esque romp 'I'm Gonna Lock My Heart (And Throw Away The Key), and the misjudged Claude Thornhill dirge 'I Wish I Had You'. These would be consistent and listenable sessions by anyone's standards, but being Billie in fine fettle, they are rather more than that; high class, jazz-inflected pop featuring the most remarkable song stylist of the day. September 1938 and she's back – sounding a tad tired perhaps – with the Basie boys infusing the jazz content into ephemeral obscurities 'I've Got A Date With A Dream' and 'You Can't Be Mine' (featuring Lester Young on clarinet and Dickie Wells on tender trombone) along with top material. 'The Very Thought Of You' is the best song by British songwriter-bandleader Ray Noble (whose others include 'The Touch Of Your Lips' and 'Goodnight Sweetheart') while 'I Can't Get Started' (featuring delicious piping horn riffs and a superb Lester solo) has survived as a standard despite the topical lyrics.

There hadn't been a Teddy Wilson session for ten months and two were organised for October and November 1938, with Billie featuring on six sides. Starring Benny Goodman's declamatory trumpet hero Harry James amid neat swing band arrangements by Benny Carter, there is an instant change in temperature. The intro to 'Everybody's Laughing' fairly guffaws out, with smooth horn riffs behind Billie and Wilson spilling and sprinkling better than ever, but the song is clumsily written and even these guys can't save it, though the cheeky 'Here It Is Tomorrow Again' fares better.

The 9 November session is memorable for featuring three of the worst songs anyone concerned had the misfortune to be associated with. The derisory 'Say It With A Kiss' was clearly knocked out by maestros Harry Warren and Johnny Mercer between proper songs, 'I'll Never Fail You' is a pitiful by-numbers piece of work, while 'April In My Heart' (Hoagy Carmichael!) is comically overcrowded and tortuous. That the musicians put such a professional gloss on these numbers only makes them all the more bewildering. Only 'They Say' comes close to being worthy of their attention, with a majestic Benny Carter solo as an added bonus.

The Quintessential Billie Holiday Volume 7
1938–1939

(CK 46180)

You're So Desirable/You're Gonna See A Lot Of
Me/Hello, My Darling/Let's Dream In The
Moonlight/That's All I Ask Of You/Dream Of
Life/What Shall I Say?/It's Easy To Blame The
Weather/More Than You Know/Sugar (That Sugar
Baby O'Mine)/You're Too Lovely To Last/Under A
Blue Jungle Moon/Everything Happens For The
Best/Why Did I Always Depend On You?/Long
Gone Blues/Some Other Spring/Our Love Is
Different

*The strained relationship between Billie and John
Hammond came to a head when Billie complained
about the quality of material Hammond had organised
for her to sing for the 28 November Wilson-led session,
with the singer even suggesting sabotage. Though Billie's
low spirits may have been affected by her leaving Artie
Shaw in distressing circumstances a week before the
session, second-rate Ray Noble ('You're So Desirable'),
nondescript Tin Pan Alley and Hollywood fare ('You're
Gonna See A Lot Of Me' and 'Let's Dream In The
Moonlight') were depressingly below par for the period
and probably didn't help. Also, the jazz obbligatos and
solos had been largely replaced by slick swing band gestures, but given the backing she went on to prefer, this
was not likely to be a problem.*

*Following a fair pair of sides under her own name (the
Chu Berry-adorned 'That's All I Ask Of You' and the
Carmen McRae-penned 'Dream Of Life'), enough bad*

*feeling had brewed between Billie and the man who dis-
covered her for Wilson's 30 January 1939 session to be
the last time Hammond ever recorded Billie Holiday.
Although never romantically involved (indeed, it is said
that Hammond rejected Billie's advances early on
which, in Billie's mind, confused things), it is tempting in
retrospect to imagine the lines from 'What Shall I Say?':
'they don't know they're not with me/What shall I say?'
resonating beyond the song.*

*It is a good session, with Roy Eldridge and Benny
Carter in particularly eloquent form and Billie skilfully
and delightfully giving herself to the contrived but cute
Cahn and Chaplin piece 'It's Easy To Blame The
Weather' and attractive 1920s stand-by 'Sugar'. The
jewel, however, is the beautiful reading of Vincent
Youmans's 'More Than You Know', which reminds us that
for all the pleasure the minor Tin Pan Alley songs can
give – especially when buffed up by Billie and company
– there is nothing quite like great artists meeting great
songs.*

*Two months after that end-of-an-era session, on 21
March 1939 Billie led (which from now on is all she ever
did) a date featuring members of the Café Society
band, cutting an unprecedented five sides. The most
arranged-sounding Holiday cuts yet, they are moody and
alluring, pointing the clear way to where she was head-
ing. Not that the material – the insipid 'You're Too Lovely
To Last', the dull 'Why Did I Always Depend on You', the
dubious Dorothy Lamour-esque exotica of 'Under A Blue
Jungle Moon' – represents such a leap in quality, but the
ordered ensembles makes the music sound all of an
atmospheric piece and Billie sounds relaxed and sexy,
particularly on 'Jungle Moon'. Billie gets a co-credit on*

'*Everything Happens For The Best*', but not much happens save a perky Tab Smith solo and a Wilson-esque contribution (weren't they all) from pianist Kenny Kersey.

The revelation came at the end-of-session filler, '*Long Gone Blues*', a second original Holiday blues that for all its restraint has remarkable power. Following a vamp chorus on the horns, Billie pitches the lines '*Talk to me baby/Tell me what's the matter now*' in such a way that leaves no doubt that here is a jazz musician at work. Sensual, capricious and highly musical, it is an amazing piece of work, proving once more that when she felt like it, Billie was a great blues singer. She had resisted Hammond's attempts to sing blues with Basie ('*Ah, hell*', she said, '*I ain't singing that old shit! This is 1938!*') yet not a year later, here she was finding her own way around new blues. Proving Columbia barely knew what they had, '*Long Gone Blues*' wasn't released until 1946 when Billie was a star and long gone from the company.

In another misjudgment, on 20 April 1939 Columbia allowed Commodore records to 'borrow' Billie for one session in order to record the remarkable song Billie was singing to such great effect at the Café Society, '*Strange Fruit*', a recording that transformed Billie's career. (For the story, see The Complete Commodore Recordings.) However, in July 1939, it was business as usual with Billie and members of the Café Society band – including current lover Sonny White on piano – back in the studio.

'*Some Other Spring*' was written by Irene Kitchings (Billie's friend and Teddy Wilson's then wife) and Arthur Herzog (a future Holiday collaborator) and in its musical richness and poetic language probably represented

*the quality of song Billie aspired to singing more regu-
larly. Certainly, she often cited it as her favourite song
and regretted it wasn't given more attention. White and
Holiday are listed among the co-composers of 'Our Love
Is Different' and while hardly in the same class as
'Spring', it contains the odd melodic surprise and has a
certain languid charm.*

The Quintessential Billie Holiday Volume 8
1939–1940

(CK 47030)

Them There Eyes/Swing, Brother, Swing/Night And
Day/The Man I Love/You're Just A No Account/
You're A Lucky Guy/Ghost Of Yesterday/Body And
Soul/What Is This Going To Get Us?/Falling In Love
Again (Can't Help It)/I'm Pulling Through/Tell Me
More And More, And Then Some/Laughing At
Life/Time On My Hands/I'm All For You/I Hear
Music/The Same Old Story/Practice Makes Perfect

*Completing the July 1939 session, these tracks prove it
wasn't all elegant indolence down at the Café Society.
'Them There Eyes' sounds like an old-style rhythm novelty with Billie happily all over the beat, but already the
rasp is getting stronger, the life she lived creeping into
her sound, though writer Ralph J Gleason detects something 'deep-throated, magnificently sexual' in her 'aaah
baby' cry. The band intro is a touch hokey and if Tab
Smith and Kenneth Hollon are not quite Benny Carter
and Lester Young, they are entertaining and Charlie
Shavers is excellent on trumpet. (Billie clearly felt this*

sliver of a song did its job well enough to still be featuring it in concert in the mid-1950s.)

The studio edition of another minimally composed tear-up, 'Swing Brother Swing', has been eclipsed by the precious aircheck version with the Count Basie Orchestra from 1938, but it holds up well enough with all the soloists generating some genuine excitement.

Billie may have said goodbye to John Hammond but she reacquainted herself in the studio with the Basie crew on 13 December 1939 for a noticeably higher class of repertoire: a Porter ('Night And Day'), a Gershwin ('The Man I Love') and a pair of hip and throwaway Cahn and Chaplins ('You're Just A No Account' and 'You're A Lucky Guy'). However, it is an oddly anonymous session, the arrangements erring toward the sweet and doleful rather than the spontaneous, swinging interplay of earlier dates. Lester and Buck Clayton get some solo space (Lester's half-chorus on 'The Man I Love' is a gem) but the emphasis is on a mid-sized backing band for Lady. Billie, more intimately recorded than ever, has extra audible grain in her voice than previously but sings with wonderful autonomy, especially on 'Night And Day', expanding and contracting the phrases with unerring instinct.

A session on 29 February 1940 continued the quest for better material as Billie turned to the writers of her current favourite 'Some Other Spring' (Irene Kitchings-Wilson and Arthur Herzog) for 'Ghost Of Yesterday' and 'What Is This Going To Get Us'. The latter is an ungainly piece with baffling modulations and muddled pronouns but 'Ghost Of Yesterday' is another intriguing, surprising song of such elegiac density it makes the popular quasi-art song of the period, 'Body And Soul', sound relatively straightforward.

Interestingly, Billie recorded 'Body And Soul' on this session as well, making it quite a heavyweight song date. She makes stylish work of Johnny Green's classic with a few sly moderations here and there, but she is essentially respectful to the composition while quietly taking it for herself. The use of two alternate stanzas for the reprise turn a thirty-two bar song into a vivid piece of storytelling. And she sang 'my life a hell you're making' rather than 'mess', which is the choice of most singers.

'Falling In Love Again' – virtually ignored since Marlene Dietrich's heavy-lidded 1930s The Blue Angel version – was an odd choice but re-cast in a relaxed 4/4, it becomes Billie's lighter, having-myself-a-time persona beautifully.

Teddy Wilson was hired as pianist for the session of 7 June 1940 and adds sparkle to the sound; one hardly realised he was missed until he was there again. The fresh-sounding 'I'm Pulling Through' is the last Irene Kitchings lyric Billie sang until 1946 (Billie soon supplanted Kitchings herself as Herzog's co-composer) and while perhaps not of the quality of 'Some Other Spring' or 'Ghost Of Yesterday', it is certainly interesting enough to make one wonder what Herzog and Kitchings could have achieved had they continued writing together.

The Holiday-credited (and Herzog-disputed) minor dirge 'Tell Me More And More, And Then Some' is actually quite an affecting piece, beautifully dealt with by Billie, spectrally floating over mournful Ellingtonian horn chords. The rhythm tune 'Laughing At Life' is like a hipper version of 'When You're Smiling' featuring a jaunty Wilson piano while Vincent Youmans's lovely 'Time On My Hands' is given a leisurely, sensual treatment by a tender-voiced Billie.

*Members of the short-lived Teddy Wilson big band joined
Billie on a September 1940 jukebox fodder recording
session, with the orderly arrangements — probably by
Don Redman — aimed at dancers. 'I'm All For You' and
'The Same Old Story' are slow and smooth while the
obscure 'Practice Makes Perfect' and the superior
Loesser and Lane piece 'I Hear Music' rattle efficiently
along, peppered by piquant interjections from old pal
Roy Eldridge and new pal, tenorist Don Byas. Billie is
professional if unmoved.*

The Quintessential Billie Holiday Volume 9
1940–1942

(CK 47031)

St Louis Blues/Loveless Love/Let's Do It/Georgia
On My Mind/Romance In The Dark/All Of Me/I'm
In A Low-Down Groove/God Bless The Child/Am I
Blue?/Solitude/Jim/I Cover The Waterfront/Love Me
Or Leave Me/Gloomy Sunday/Wherever You
Are/Mandy Is Two/It's A Sin To Tell A Lie/Until The
Real Thing Comes Along

*The two tunes recorded with orchestra under the direc-
tion of Benny Carter on 15 October 1940 were W C
Handy's 'St Louis Blues' and 'Loveless Love', intended as
a John Hammond and Leonard Feather-conceived tribute to the Father Of The Blues. It was never completed
but Billie's surviving sides once more display her melodic touch with blues material.*

On 'St Louis Blues', in an ingenious and undoubtedly

instinctive twist by the singer, where Handy's tune calls for blues phrases (in the first and second stanzas) Billie substitutes melodic styling, where he calls for melody (in the fourth stanza 'Got the St Louis Blues...' Billie substitutes the lowest-down moaning blues lines she had yet committed to wax.) So authoritative is she on these tracks that while one understands her reluctance to revisit an idiom that was already considered by some to be old-fashioned, it is regretful that she wasn't inclined at this stage in her development to further explore the blues in general and Handy's oeuvre in particular.

Café Society pianist Eddie Heywood joins four horns (including Lester Young, who hardly gets a look in) and three other rhythm players for Billie's tautly arranged date on 21 March 1941. Billie's take on Cole Porter's suggestive 'Let's Do It' is a perfect example of her ability to stretch the timing of a line – particularly noticeable with some of Porter's wordy strings ('goldfish in the privacy of bowls do it') – so far behind the beat, it sounds like she's on the verge of being caught out. Of course, she never is. 'Georgia On My Mind' is a marvellous illustration of Billie's mature note choices being as sophisticated and poignant as a horn player's, perhaps – as several commentators (including Miles Davis) have pointed out – those of two horn players in particular, Lester Young and Louis Armstrong.

'All Of Me' is not so consistently inventive as 'Georgia On My Mind' but at least one of her variations (to be exact, the 9th she substitutes for the root at the end of the second line 'why not take all of me') has passed into common currency via Frank Sinatra's 1954 version (who uses it on 'eyes that cry' in the second half of the tune). 'Romance In The Dark' is, by contrast, a run-of-the-mill rhythm tune but in this form, Billie having the most routine of fun is still a delight and Heywood delivers an attractively crisp solo.

Heywood was the piano man again on 9 May 1941, for a similar-sounding date (without the rhythm tune), this time without Lester but with Roy Eldridge added. 'I'm In A Low-Down Groove' is a hugely attractive torch song ripe for rediscovery; Eldridge produces some warm, muted encouragement following some oddly inappropriate perky brass ensembles while Billie keeps her head well above despair with it. Which is more than can be said for 'Am I Blue?' and 'Solitude', all wearying, long-held high notes and curtains of woeful horns. 'Solitude' fares better because it is Ellington, but the peach of the session is 'God Bless The Child', Holiday and Herzog's touching, jumbled piece of homespun philosophy.

Billie's penultimate session for Columbia in August 1941 was a good one, centring once more around the unruffled musicianship of the man who was there from the beginning, Teddy Wilson. 'Jim' is an exemplary, clear-eyed reading of a contemporary pop tune of the my-mean-man-how-I-love-him sort and Billie's growing empathy with this kind of material is obvious, though she keeps her dignity here, singing it rather splendidly. She does the same quality job on 'I Cover The Waterfront', a superior song written after the film of the same name and remaining forever associated with Billie. 'Love Me Or Leave Me', like 'Waterfront', dates from a previous decade, and Billie has fun with the octave leaps in the melody, playing will-she-won't-she throughout. Both sides are further characterised by the unusual presence of the verses.

The most extraordinary side of the August 1941 session is 'Gloomy Sunday', a Hungarian tune with an English lyric that contemplates suicide following the death of a loved one, promoted as the 'Hungarian Suicide Song'. 'Let them not weep/Let them know that I'm glad to go,' wails Billie, 'Death is no dream for in death I'm caressing you' before that tell-tale change to the major tonality and 'Dream/I was only dreaming'. For all its corny manipulation, 'Gloomy Sunday' remains a fabulously effective performance (and one of Billie's personal favourites) due not least to the keening tenor of Billie's vocal, but also to the tugging minor harmonies in the composition. The gloomy postscript to this strange tale is that the composer, Rezso Seress, did indeed commit suicide in 1968.

Billie's final session for Columbia on 10 February 1942 led with a feeble if harmless salute to the US soldiers overseas, 'Wherever You Are'. It was rendered doubly pointless by the fact that it and the other sides from the session remained unreleased by Columbia until after the war. 'Mandy Is Two' is a sweet, shamelessly sentimental song about a growing little girl. That it is sung so touchingly by a childless woman – who, according to those close to her, yearned for motherhood – can't help but add to the poignancy. Critic Benny Green cites it as a perfect example of Billie 'endowing any old jingle with the grace of art'. The piously silly 'It's A Sin To Tell A Lie' was never the same after Fats Waller got a hold of it, thank goodness, and Billie wafts through the song, negotiating it with some care but no particular purpose. The final cut – 'Until The Real Thing Comes Along' – is more like it and Billie is there body and soul.

The first nine years of Billie's recording career

produced a delightful if daunting body of work. For those wishing to sample this period in less distinctive form, there are a few options. There is a three-disc, handsomely packaged seventy-track condensation of the period on The Legacy *(Columbia 469049), which in offsetting the studio sides with airshots and examples of controversial later work from 1958, produces an odd balance.*

Of the many budget releases of this material, ABM have produced five CDs called The Incomparable, *volumes 1 to 5, condensing the period down to 100 sides including the four sides from the first Commodore session of 1939 and the rare, quickly withdrawn Artie Shaw side 'Any Old Time'. The packaging is unglamorous but the sound is comparable to the* Quintessential *series and one cannot deny the value.* Love Songs *(Columbia Legacy 483878 2) is a sixteen-track compilation of some famous, though not necessarily characteristic titles; the nature of the theme means classic performances like 'Mean To Me' and sassy period obscurities like 'Having Myself A Time' are absent. Look out for the next generation of Columbia's repackaging of this essential music.*

The Complete Commodore Recordings 1939–1944 2 Disc Set

(CMD-2-401)

The Commodore Master Takes
Strange Fruit (2 takes)/Yesterdays (2 takes)/Fine and Mellow/I Gotta Right To Sing The Blues (2 takes)/ How Am I To Know (4 takes)/My Old Flame (4 takes)/I'll Get By (2 takes)/I Cover The Waterfront (4 takes)/I'll Be Seeing You (3 takes)/

I'm Yours (3 takes)/ Embraceable You (3 takes)/As Time Goes By (2 takes)/He's Funny That Way (5 takes)/Lover Come Back To Me (4 takes)/Billie's Blues (3 takes)/On The Sunny Side Of The Street

Milt Gabler was a jazz enthusiast who ran a record shop in midtown Manhattan and organised jam sessions to stimulate work for musicians. He was the first record man to reissue jazz records (purchasing out-of-print pressings from record companies) and founded Commodore Records in 1938 as a way of recording the music he loved, often played by the musicians who had taken to hanging around his shop. By the time Commodore folded in the mid-1950s, 64 LPs'-worth of music by the greatest musicians of the era had been recorded (released in its entirety by Mosaic records in the late 1980s). Billie's relationship with Gabler and Commodore began in 1939 when the singer came into his store on West 52nd St complaining that Columbia would not let her record 'Strange Fruit'.

'Strange Fruit' was the startling song depicting a lynching scene that had grabbed Billie and was dumbfounding the audiences at the Café Society. Openly provocative in its graphic descriptions, Columbia regarded the song as too hot to handle and as they had a good relationship with Gabler (processing and pressing his records), gave Billie leave to record a single session with him.

Gathering the Café Society band, including Frankie Newton (trumpet), Tab Smith, Kenneth Hollon (reeds) and Sonny White (piano) on 20 April 1939, Billie and Gabler set about recording this remarkable piece, presumably just as it was heard at the Café Society. It opens with portentous, dour tones from the horns and a disorientating whole-tone line from Newton on muted trumpet, then murmuring minor arpeggiated chords from the piano that linger far longer than the listener expects. Billie doesn't make her first entrance until over a minute into the song. That would not be so surprising in itself if the band had been playing a theme, but all they do is set a disquietingly mournful mood until the singer is ready to deliver her message.

Already hooked, from the moment this strange, sad voice intones the opening lines 'Southern trees bear a strange fruit/Blood on the leaves and blood at the root', the listener is engaged at a different level. Musically, not much happens – the melody and harmonies drift aimlessly and forlornly around the minor tonality (which has a disturbingly confusing impact in itself) – but dramatically speaking, 'Strange Fruit' is a shattering experience. The harrowing images are presented dispassionately, with just a tiny twist of sneering irony when appropriate ('pastoral scene of the gallant south'). In a display of masterful theatrical command, Billie allows the lyric to do its job with an extraordinary sense of sad power-in-reserve. The heat of anger, pain and sorrow is felt rather than heard.

Despite being banned from most radio stations, 'Strange Fruit' was coupled with another tune from the session – 'Fine And Mellow' – which was popular on the jukeboxes and became the equivalent of a Top Twenty hit. 'Fine And Mellow' was another original blues that Gabler encouraged her to do because he'd loved her 'Billie's Blues' from July 1936 so much. Although Gabler arranged it to approximate old-style blues ('rambling piano and Frankie Newton's muted trumpet, like Joe Smith would play behind Bessie Smith', recalled Gabler) he also rated it as 'the first modern blues session, really'. Interestingly, 'Fine And Mellow' is a more straightforward blues performance from Billie than 'Billie's Blues', with much earthy wailing on bent 'blue' notes in contrast to the more measured, melodic approach of the earlier cut. Although he had helped with the lyrics himself, including the verse that produced the title, Gabler registered the copyright solely in Billie's name, ensuring life-long royalties for the singer.

Billie irons out those troublesome climbing scalar phrases on 'Yesterdays', a difficult Jerome Kern song with archaic lyrics by Otto Harbach. While Billie doesn't quite convince us she understands everything she's singing (rather than 'forsooth' she sings 'then sooth', which may, in fact, be better), it is nevertheless a poignant performance — especially the slow chorus before the tempo change — and has been cited by Billie as one of her all-time favourite songs.

'I Gotta Right To Sing The Blues' is a glorious 'happy blues' performance of the fine Arlen-Koehler song, the highlight being Billie's bridging phrase between the two halves: 'Mi-se-ry-ee-I gotta right to sing the blues...' Harold Arlen's sophisticated, bluesy style of composition really suited Billie and she got round to singing several more of his songs in the 1950s. The band get a chance to stretch out for the only time in the session (specifically Smith on lively alto and White on scurrying piano) and there is a rare sense — given this was Billie's current working band rather than a Wilson-led pick-up band — that we are hearing what we would hear if we were at a club at the time. This, along with the precious documentation of 'Strange Fruit' makes the first Commodore session of April 1939 particularly valuable.

Left A rare shot of Holiday aged three, *c.* 1918.

Below The Cotton Club, the legendary home of New York blues.

Right A fresh-faced early publicity shot.

Below In performance.

Left and below Although notoriously erratic in her attendance of recording sessions, Holiday was never more at home than in front of the microphone.

Left With Louis Armstrong, c. 1941.

Below With band leader Duke Ellington, c. 1950.

Left Holiday's conviction for substance abuse meant she was denied the chance to perform in New York's nightclubs. Instead, the world of theatres and dancehalls became her new home.

Right With husband Louis McKay, who brought a certain amount of stability into Holiday's life.

Above *c.* 1952, at a happier period of her life.

Right Performing at The Royal Albert Hall, London during her triumphant European tour, 1954.

Lady Day

There was a sense that for all Billie's growing reputation on the Café Society scene she had somehow missed out capitalising on the Swing boom (despite the occasional effective rhythm track) in the way that Ella Fitzgerald and others had. For all her artistry and burgeoning profile as 'Queen of 52nd Street' during the war years, she was considered by some — including, clearly, Columbia — as a tricky customer: not just personally (though her growing reputation in that area would not have helped) but musically too. She was just too 'artistic', as Artie Shaw's management once called her. In the wake of the American Federation Of Musicians recording ban of August 1942 (they were holding out for broadcast fees and the strike lasted over a year), Columbia didn't renew Billie's contract. Once more, she turned to her old friend Milt Gabler who was delighted to help, commissioning pianist and Café Society bandleader Eddie Heywood to do a dozen arrangements and booking three sessions in March and April 1944.

The Commodore sides are all delightful and the clearest effort yet to guide Billie's music in a jazz-inflected pop direction. The arrangements are functional and do little more than stay out of Billie's way, but the songs (chosen by Gabler) are high quality and Billie is in top form, plaintive but resonant. Tellingly, several of the songs are set in the slowest tempos Billie had yet recorded (often at odds, interestingly, with Heywood's solo piano intros). The obscure but lovely 'How Am I To Know' and the war-years lament 'I'll Be Seeing You' both conspicuously dawdle in comparison with many of the Columbia sides and rather than making Billie sound 'less' behind the beat as one might expect, it simply gives her more room to play with the phrasing.

Billie had already recorded 'I Cover The Waterfront' in August 1941 on one of her last Columbia sessions but it had yet to be released when she re-made it for Gabler. Only two and a half years apart, the performances make for an interesting comparison. The backing on the 1944 version is several notches slower and less rhythmically explicit, the vocal phrasing is wider and the rallentando coda is more elaborately handled. Every element of the music is manipulated to heighten the dramatic nature of the piece.

'Embraceable You' goes the same vivid way to luscious effect, though the delightful Harburg and Green obscurity 'I'm Yours', 'As Time Goes By' and another remake, 'He's Funny That Way', though beautiful ballad performances, succeed without resorting to the alluring crawling tempos used elsewhere.

The final Commodore session favours medium tempo numbers and Billie re-shapes 'Lover Come Back To Me', 'On The Sunny Side Of The Street' and her own 'Billie's Blues' (an entirely different set of melodic choices to the 1936 version) with by-now customary expertise.

The Complete Commodore Recordings contains the earliest set of extensive Billie Holiday alternate takes available to us (stretching sixteen titles over forty-five tracks) which, while having its own peculiar magnetic pull through the listening, reveals a surprising consistency. Far from being the freewheeling improviser of melodic variations that one might imagine, Billie is often revealed as having a 'conception' of how she is going to sing a song, varying her approach from take to take only in the smallest of details, even on a vehicle like 'Billie's Blues'. In the absence of any notable jazz soloing, only serious students of the minutiae of Billie's singing or

Eddie Heywood's dainty (if faintly banal) piano intros will require The Complete *set; most listeners will be satisfied with the sixteen excellent sides on* The Commodore Master Takes.

The Complete Decca Recordings 1944–1950
2 Disc Set

(GRD2-601)

Lover Man (Oh Where Can You Be?)/No More (2 takes)/That Ole Devil Called Love/Don't Explain (2 versions)/Big Stuff (4 versions)/You Better Go Now/What Is This Thing Called Love/Good Morning Heartache/No Good Man (2 takes)/Baby I Don't Cry Over You (2 takes)/I'll Look Around (2 takes)/The Blues Are Brewin'/Guilty (3 takes)/Easy Living/Solitude (2 takes)/Weep No More/Girls Were Made To Take Care Of Boys/I Love You Porgy/My Man (2 takes)/'Tain't Nobody's Business If I Do/Baby Get Lost/Keep On A-Rainin'/Them There Eyes/Do Your Duty/Gimme A Pigfoot (And A Bottle Of Beer)/You Can't Lose A Broken Heart/My Sweet Hunk O' Trash/Now Or Never/You're My Thrill/Crazy He Calls Me/Please Tell Me Now/Somebody's On My Mind/God Bless The Child/This Is Heaven To Me

With the Commodore recordings, Milt Gabler was resolutely steering Billie down the torchy pop road, convinced that was where she belonged. When he heard Billie sing 'Lover Man', Gabler was so struck by its commercial potential he felt he had no choice but to sign

Billie to Decca to make pop records. On 4 October 1944, with Holiday-requested strings arranged by Toots Camarata, they recorded 'Lover Man' and Camarata's original 'No More'.

The arrangement of 'Lover Man' is discreet and rather attractive, but Billie's vocal of forthright erotic yearning is masterful, ranking with the peak of her achievements. An unusual composition, with composed bluesy phrases and risqué lyrics, it was a national hit; with the singer's barely veiled sensual hunger thrust into the mainstream, Billie Holiday became a name. 'My big thrill', recalled Gabler, 'was to take a great artist and match them with a song and have it become a standard'. With Billie Holiday and 'Lover Man', he did just that.

The recording of 'No More' from the same session showed that if this was going to be Billie's shot at pop success, she wasn't going to be recording just fluff. Camarata's arty tone poem of a song is Ellingtonian in its density and Bob Russell (a successful sometime Ellington lyricist) does a fine job of making this rangy, elusive piece memorable. Billie once again sounds untroubled by the odd intervals, turning in a skilled, moving recital. (The rare alternate take – revealing her sliding less convincingly between notes – proves that this kind of performance did not just happen.)

In the four sessions scheduled between November 1944 and March 1946 Billie cut just seven new titles including two of her most famous tunes, 'That Ole Devil Called Love' and 'Don't Explain'. The former was a piece of superior pop that appeared as the flip side to 'Lover Man' and may be familiar to contemporary listeners through Alison Moyet's carbon copy remake of 1985.

Feminists point to 'Don't Explain' as a classic

example of the kind of woman-as-doormat song female vocalists should move on from: 'you're my joy and pain' whines Billie, helplessly, 'I'm glad you're back'. Too true, and yet technically the piece itself is striking and hard to fault as well as being a moving portrayal of an all-too-common kind of emotional dependency – one which, after all, Billie suffered from in one way or another throughout her life. Whether it should be so beautifully celebrated in song is another question.

Sessions were not as productive as they should have been and Gabler admits that around this time Billie was 'becoming a little more difficult to work with' which is hardly surprising, distracted as she was by her new man Joe Guy and a substantial heroin habit. However, it does not always appear to have been entirely her fault, especially during the extraordinary 'Big Stuff' episode.

Decca planned to release a four-disc version of 'Fancy Free' by hot new broadway composer Leonard Bernstein, as recorded by the American Ballet Theatre, with the prologue – 'Big Stuff' – reserved for Billie. Attempts at all four sessions between November 1944 and March 1944 were unsuccessful for various reasons (lyrics were re-written, Bernstein objected to an inter-jected note of Billie's, other takes were rejected on unknown grounds) until Billie with a quintet (which had been reduced from full orchestra) finally nailed it on a single-side, three-and-a-half-hour session. True, it was a rambling, imaginative and subtle piece, but given that she captured 'No More' in an hour, it is clear things were going awry.

Billie had heard 'You Better Go Now' (from the 1936 musical New Faces) sung in the 'graceful parlando' of British-born cabaret artist Mabel Mercer, and a robust arrangement by Bob Haggart along with a lovely performance from Billie make it one of the classic Decca sides. (Sarah Vaughan named it as her all-time favourite Billie Holiday cut.) A 1929 Cole Porter standard 'What Is This Thing Called Love' is given a genuinely relaxed recital on the same session (14 August 1945) and one is struck at just how good the tempos are for Billie on the Decca sessions. Featuring rare (for Decca) and engaging instrumental solos from trumpeter Bill Stegmeyer and guitarist Tiny Grimes and smoothly swinging ensembles, this cut sounds like Billie coming home.

Billie often said that if she didn't feel it, she couldn't sing it. 'If you find a tune and it's got something to do with you,' she explained, 'you don't have to evolve anything. You just feel it, and when you sing it other people can feel it too...give me a song I can feel, and it's never work'. Increasingly, other than the occasional 'new love' piece, it seems the songs she could 'feel' were downbeat tunes about helpless, even unhealthy love and general disappointment and heartache. 'She would sing for losers,' as Gabler had it, and he took positive steps to perpetuate the style, commissioning Billie's friend Irene 'Some Other Spring' Kitchings (now Higginbotham) to fashion a pair of unlucky-in-love songs with Dan Fisher. They came up with a couple of tailor-made gems in 'Good Morning Heartache' and 'No Good Man'.

'Heartache' is archetypal Decca-era Billie; elegantly dressed resignation, an acknowledgement of persistently familiar misery that borders on the affectionate. The central conceit of almost personifying the relentless despair that stalks the singer is brilliantly sustained and presented with a beautiful lightness of touch from both

vocalist and arranger (Bill Stegmeyer), with the threatened mawkishness sidestepped with ease. 'No Good
Man', despite comparable compositional and performance values, fares slightly less well due simply to the
uncomfortable 'I ought to hate him yet I love him' subject matter. Interestingly, upon release Metronome
reviewed the sides in prophetic warning tones: 'There's a
danger that Billie's present formula will wear thin, but up
to now it's wearing well.'

The strings were dropped for the 9 April 1946 session
which produced two relaxed head arrangement quintet
performances of 'Baby I Don't Cry Over You' and 'I'll Look
Around', two heartening songs of survival. 'Baby' is a
sassy, defiant number, while 'Around' is a sweet, har-
monically rambling song written by Billie admirers
George Cory and Douglas Cross. (Gabler remembers
'they used to follow her around and be like gofers for her
– see that she got up in the morning, that she got to the
club, you know'.) Later, they were to write the considerably duller, infinitely more successful 'I Left My Heart In
San Francisco'.

Following Billie's appearance in the movie New
Orleans, on 27 December 1946 she recorded – from
the film – 'The Blues Are Brewin'', an interesting, song-
writerly take on the blues featuring a ten-bar blues as
its basis, plus an eight-bar bridge. That makes it about
as authentic as the 'story of jazz' film for which it was
written. The rest of the session was taken up with
recording 'Guilty', a 1931 Richard Whiting-Gus Kahn
song the publishers were trying to revive. Despite a good
arrangement and a careful, detailed vocal from Billie,
Gabler was dissatisfied with the result, recording it later
with Ella Fitzgerald. That the session was regarded as a

failure is indicated by the fact that neither track received immediate release; 'Brewin'' was delayed for five years, 'Guilty' did not appear until 1958.

The 13 February 1947 session was more productive, with four quality sides cut. 'Deep Song' was another adventurous Cory–Cross mood piece, especially written for Billie's noir-songs-for-losers persona, and if the 1936 Isham Jones standard 'There Is No Greater Love' doesn't quite justify the crawling tempo it is set in, the arranger on the date, Bob Haggart, was impressed with how Billie handled the bridge. 'An excellent example of how Billie could take a standard tune,' he commented, 'and add her Midas touch to the existing melody – giving the song a whole new value'. The session was completed with two re-makes – 'Easy Living' and 'Solitude'. Ten and six years on from the respective earlier versions, the leisurely tempos and masterly delivery of the Decca sides mark them as superior readings, marginally perhaps with respect to 'Easy Living' but significantly as far as 'Solitude' is concerned. Mature, relaxed, technically controlled, for all her problems, Billie Holiday was simply at her vocal peak in the 1940s.

She was also at her personal nadir. Before her next appearance in a recording studio sixteen months later, she had gone 'cold turkey' in a clinic to no avail before spending ten months from May 1947 until March 1948 in prison for possession, returning to sold-out Carnegie Hall concerts but also to a renewed drug habit. She completely failed to show for a recording session scheduled for 22 October 1948 and was billed for the cost. Gabler must have been anxious when Billie was 'very late' (as pianist Bobby Tucker remembers) for the 10 December 1948 session, but at last she arrived to participate in a fascinating date.

Gordon Jenkins and Tom Adair's 'Weep No More' was obviously chosen (probably even written) to capitalise on the blazing publicity surrounding Billie's private life. Decca did not hang on to this one, it was in the shops within a month of recording and the first new words Billie's slavering public heard her sing on disc were these: 'I'm just about fed up/I've finally had my fill/Of sitting round crying in my beer/I've drunk the bitter cup/I've downed the bitter pill/While waiting for the silver lining to appear.' At this point vocal group The Stardusters wah-wah some comical period backing as Billie sings 'I'm going to stack my blues up/On the very highest shelf/I'm going to pack my blues up/And get wise to myself.' 'Weep No More' virtually amounts to a post-prison press release.

The other Stardusters-adorned cut — Ralph Blane's disgraceful 'Girls Were Made To Take Care Of Boys' — is a nauseous subservient female song that entirely lacks the gritty love-as-sickness quality Billie usually invests in such material. She would make up for that with the rest of the session. In an apparently spontaneous move, The Stardusters were dismissed and Bobby Tucker and Billie came up with a lightening adaptation of Gershwin's lament from Porgy and Bess, 'I Love You Porgy'. Ingeniously modifying the opera's duet into a lovesick monologue and losing the Aunt Jemimaisms, it's one of Billie's great story-song moments, as is the other head arrangement they devised, a remake of 'My Man'.

Immeasurably superior to her 1937 version and considerably more disturbing due to the inclusion of masochistic lyrics ('He isn't true/He beats me too/What am I to do'), 'My Man' is an electrifying listen. Delivered with such a measured sense of timing (the verse is the slowest, most out-of-tempo piece she had ever recorded and Tucker responds with great empathy) and such vivid nuance of expression, it is the sort of performance that has fans and commentators routinely saying 'she sings like she's lived every line'. As we have seen, she did not always 'live every line'; sometimes she just did a professional, somewhat disconnected job of singing. Increasingly, however, from this point, the what-you-hear-is-who-I-am aspect to her music is inescapable. And given the distressing subject matter of 'My Man' ('leave him!' we shout pointlessly, as so many of her friends did in her life), it is not always a comfortable experience.

A further arrest (and subsequent acquittal) and various other well-publicised difficulties ('Billie In Trouble Again' went one Down Beat cover) contributed to Billie's 17 August 1948 recording of Bessie Smith's 1923 hit "Tain't Nobody's Business If I Do' sounding like further Billie Holiday autobiographical manifesto-as-song. 'If my man ain't got no money/And I say take all of mine honey…Well I'd rather my man hit me/Than for him to jump up and quit me/Ain't nobody's business if I do'. Down Beat referred to this kind of personalised repertoire as 'embarrassingly pertinent'.

Almost as if in response to such an oddly joyous expression of misguided loyalty and painful dependence, Leonard Feather (one of Billie's friends who looked on horrified at the mess she had made around herself) penned a lippy, sexily defiant blues for her – 'Baby Get Lost' – to record at the same session. She delivers the lines 'Don't want no trouble/I've got to be the boss/And if you can't play it my way/Well now baby get lost' with real sass, relishing getting her own back on her two-faced poppa; 'I'd try to stop your cheatin'/But I just don't have the time/Cause I got so many men/That they're standing right in line'. In penning those spirited lines for her, Feather sounds like he is willing Billie to fight back.

Billie (or Gabler) seemed to be on a Bessie Smith kick in this period, following ''Tain't Nobody's Business If I Do' with another three Bessie-related tunes. Some commentators have suggested a Bessie tribute album was in the pipeline, but Gabler says not. 'Keep On A-Rainin'' was actually the flip side of Bessie's ''Tain't Nobody's Business' in 1923 and on Billie's version, the band – as directed by Sy Oliver – play up the bump 'n' grind while Lady delivers a beautifully restrained vocal that recalls Duke Ellington's comment: 'As an artist, as a person, to see or hear, Lady Day was the "essence" of cool'.

'Do Your Duty' and 'Gimme A Pigfoot And A Bottle Of Beer' were written for Bessie Smith by Wesley 'Sox' Wilson and recorded at her last session in 1933 (produced by John Hammond, three days before Billie's first recording session) and continue the trend of assertive 'strong' songs that appeared to attract Billie as much as the 'defiant victim' items around this time. 'Do Your Duty' is an innuendo-laden series of demands of a feckless man while 'Pigfoot' is the sound of Billie getting some good dirty fun out of life again, though the reference to 'reefers' that appears in Bessie's version is judiciously absent from Billie's. She growls lasciviously through both performances, hamming it up more than usual, using the increased grain in her sound to marvellous effect. At this point and on this material, it suited her.

30 September 1949 saw her teamed with her childhood idol Louis Armstrong on a pair of songs from the contemporary musical Sugar Hill composed by great

stride pianist James P Johnson. 'You Can't Lose A Broken Heart' has Louis and Billie delivering separate choruses on a workmanlike song and must rank among the dullest things either had sung. 'My Sweet Hunk O' Trash', on the other hand, is organised so Billie can affection-ately lambast her no-good man while Louis giggles and pleads innocence. It's pretty entertaining but lacks a cer-tain chemistry and fine comic timing to be entirely con-vincing. The banter even gets out of hand – at one point Louis appears to say 'Fuck 'em, baby', apropos of noth-ing. It was in the shops a month before a couple of com-plaints crept out and it was withdrawn. Billie cut a rock-ing R&B novelty, 'Now Or Never', at the same time, on which she gets a composing credit. Very much period juke-box fodder, Billie rasps her way through the riffy tune with something approaching commitment and pro-duces the highlight of the session.

Gordon Jenkins was musical director for Billie's final two sessions at Decca, and on 19 October 1949 brought back strings to Billie's music for the first time since 1946, doing a lovely, lush job. 'Gordon was crazy about Billie', remembered Gabler, 'it was like having Tchaikovsky and half a symphony orchestra behind you when you sang in front of Gordon Jenkins'. Billie rose to the occasion with style. 'You're My Thrill' is an intriguing Jay Gorney–Sidney Clare song of relatively healthy-sounding physical involvement and recalls the moodily elusive sides Billie cut at the beginning of her Decca tenure. 'Crazy He Calls Me' is a Carl Sigman-composed pop song of the superior, memorable kind, while, sadly, 'Please Tell Me Now' isn't.

'Somebody's On My Mind' is credited to Holiday–Herzog (and claimed by Bobby Tucker as partly his) but remains much less well known than their 'Don't Explain' or 'God Bless The Child'. Less obviously memorable than either, it still has a certain something and deserves wider attention. Billie allows more of what Whitney Balliett called her 'laughlike staccato notes' to creep in, but it is a sweet performance of an under-exposed song.

On 8 March 1950, Billie joined Gordon Jenkins in a Hollywood recording studio for what would turn out to be her final Decca session. As the Gordon Jenkins Singers piously moo the infamous introduction to the 1950 remake of 'God Bless The Child' ('Mama may have/Poppa may have...') it is hard not to smile at such a lapse of judgement. 'I wasn't even on the West Coast when it was made,' apologises Gabler, 'I was stuck in New York. I would have killed that introduction.' Gabler was an admirer of Jenkins – 'he had such taste' – but admitted 'the only thing he didn't have was a black taste for that intro – and it doesn't belong there.' The heavenly angels and flutes don't give up for the whole side and by the time the church bells are sounding at the close, Holiday and Jenkins almost have you thinking you have been listening to a hymn.

'Child' is invaluable, peculiarly appealing kitsch that, amazingly, sounds like a model of hipness compared to the flip side, 'This Is Heaven To Me', with Billie somehow managing to convince us in lofty, quasi-spiritual terms that she is just where she wants to be. There is a very real sense of what Billie's friend and singer Carmen McRae meant when she observed: 'singing is the only place she can express herself the way she'd like to be all the time.' That, plus the corny peacefulness of the composition, adds up to quite a powerful piece. And it is hard to deny the resonance of the lines: 'Long as *freedom grows/I wanna seek it/If it's yes or no/It's me who'll speak it'. There is magic at work here.*

While the two-disc set The Complete Decca Recordings *is excellently presented and easily digested with the 'alternate' takes both kept to a sensible level and often instructive and fascinating (the 'Big Stuff' episode, for example), some listeners will prefer to sample this music away from the sometimes stultifying detail that goes into sets like this. There are many Decca-era compilations available under the banner of MCA/GRP, such as the budget* Priceless Jazz Collection.*

During the two years following her final session for Decca, Billie only recorded four sides — in April 1951 for the R&B label Aladdin — but it was a short-lived association. The tracks, a cool 'Blue Turning Grey Over You' (written by Fats Waller and recorded by Louis Armstrong, among others), a good quality ballad 'Detour Ahead' and a pair of R&B flavoured cuts, 'Be Fair With Me Baby' and 'Rocky Mountain Blues' are hard to trace on CD, but are just about due for public domain release.

THE NORMAN GRANZ YEARS

The following music can all be found unless stated on The Complete Billie Holiday On Verve 1945–1959 (10 discs)

Disc I
Jazz At The Philharmonic Concerts 1945–1947

Body And Soul/Strange Fruit/I Cried For You/Fine And Mellow/He's Funny That Way/The Man I Love/Gee Baby, Ain't I Good To You?/All Of Me/Billie's Blues/Trav'lin' Light/He's Funny That Way/You Better Go Now/You're Driving Me Crazy/There Is No Greater Love/I Cover The Waterfront

The recorded association between Granz and Billie began on 12 February 1945 at the Philharmonic Auditorium, Los Angeles, when she guested at the JATP concert to sing 'Body And Soul', effortlessly re-designing the tune while staying connected to the emotional thrust of the song (the highlight being her inspired melodic variation of 'my life a hell you're making...'). There is the notorious JATP scuffle of obbligatos between her phrases as trumpeter Howard McGhee, altoist Willie Smith and pianist (probably) Milt Raskin jostle for space to present their complimentary lines, though they are sufficiently off-mike to create minimal disruption to Billie's flow. 'Strange Fruit', thankfully, is delivered with suitably stark accompaniment (piano and bass only). It is odd to hear Billie introduce it as 'a tune that was written especially for me...I really hope you like it', like it is just another song in the set, before delivering a focused performance of chilling torment. Granz remembered Billie's face was wet with tears as she ended.

1946 saw JATP's New York concert debuts with Billie as Granz's special guest at Carnegie Hall on 27 May. A breezy, routinely buoyant 'I Cried For You' is followed by a

roar of delighted recognition for the first line ('My man don't love me…') of 'Fine And Mellow'. Interestingly, the instrumentalists do not get to solo in Billie's spot, just obbligato. As the players include Buck Clayton and Lester Young, these are performed with the greatest of discretion, particularly Lester's work on 'He's Funny That Way'.

Better recorded is the 3 June 1946 concert featuring a good 'The Man I Love' a jumbled-with-horns 'All Of Me' and 'Billie's Blues' featuring Billie's current beau Joe Guy on neat swing-to-bop trumpet obbligatos. The most interesting side of the date is a song that she had not recorded before, 'Gee Baby Ain't I Good To You', a great Redman and Razaf tune, full of the kind of smeary blues cadences that agree with Billie perfectly.

Apart from a lovely trombone intro on his own 'Trav'lin' Light' from Trummy Young on the 7 October 1946 date at LA, the horns stay out of the way for this and yet another (though entirely different) 'He's Funny That Way', both being delightful piano (Ken Kersey) and voice performances. ('She doesn't need horns,' observed Miles Davis once, 'she sounds like one anyway'.)

The same goes for the four songs sang unbilled at Carnegie Hall on 24 May 1947, with just Billie and Bobby Tucker at the piano (in immaculately responsive form as ever) presenting highly elegant readings of 'You'd Better Go Now' (released a year earlier on Decca), 'You're Driving Me Crazy' (never recorded before), 'There Is No Greater Love' (just released on Decca and receiving a rush of fresh recognition from the Carnegie Hall audience) and 'I Cover The Waterfront' (recorded for Okeh in 1941 and Commodore in 1944 and audibly requested by several members of the *audience). Considering this appearance occurred only five days after her arrest for possession of narcotics (and three days before her hearing and subsequent imprisonment), Billie gives a remarkably poised and touching performance, betraying not a hint of her troubles.*

These live performances of 1945/46/47, along with her 1957 Newport Jazz Festival set, can also be found on Billie Holiday: Jazz At The Philharmonic (Verve 521 642-2).

Los Angeles Studio Session (1952)

East Of The Sun/Blue Moon/You Go To My Head/You Turned The Tables On Me/Easy To Love/These Foolish Things/I Only Have Eyes For You/Solitude

The late spring of 1952 saw Billie's first official session for Norman Granz. His JATP records had become among the most popular in the country and he was convinced that the same kind of semi-organised spontaneity was the way forward for Billie. He booked some favourite musicians – the Oscar Peterson trio featuring Peterson on piano, Barney Kessel on guitar and Ray Brown on bass plus Flip Phillips on tenor, Charlie Shavers on trumpet and Alvin Stroller on drums – to congregate around her.

The backing works fine, but the thing the listener has to deal with here is the sound of Billie's voice. Granz liked the voice recorded closely and big in the mix in the early 1950s (compare these sessions with the Fred Astaire ones of the same year) and in these circumstances there is no escaping how she has changed since we last heard her. 'Sounds as if twenty years had passed, not just two,' notes Will Friedwald.

Discernably weathered and appearing to operate on minimum breath power with a kind of cracking howl when she chooses to hold a full note (which isn't that often) and a distinctive chuckling hiccup in place of certain kinds of pitching ('...West "of" the moon...'). And yet, once the ear has adjusted to this eccentric sound, once one stops expecting to hear 'singing' as one imagines singing should sound, there is much to enjoy in this rich period of recording. After all, as Joel E Siegal points out, her voice was 'never an instrument of remarkable range or intrinsic beauty', and with her timing and emotional reading of a lyric not only intact but more profound, many connoisseurs actually prefer the darker, deeper sides of the Granz years to Billie's previous work.

Weakened instrument or not, Granz was also keen for Billie to interpret some new songs, a process Billie was not always interested in, though he appears to have got half of his own way for the first session, which features four tunes Billie had recorded before (but were by no means overexposed) and four that she hadn't. 'East Of The Sun' and 'Blue Moon' set the tone for the majority of the Granz Years approach; conversational singing, easy, swinging rhythm section, relaxed obbligatos and robust soloing. Tempos are gorgeous, Flip Phillips is a model of Lester-like inventive discretion behind Billie's delightful vocal on 'Sun', and if trumpeter Charlie Shavers's open-horned solos sounds a shade out of keeping with the character of the groove (and like Henry 'Red' Allen's work in February 1937, has attracted some criticism), it is no more full-bodied than many of Roy Eldridge's esteemed, vigorous contributions to Billie's Columbia sides.

The horns lay out on 'You Go To My Head' which features some delicious supportive guitar work from Barney Kessel and is a drop or two more intoxicated than Billie's 1938 reading of the song. It also features the first of Oscar Peterson's several surprising ending chords, which lend a pleasing tone of gentle modernism to the session. 'You Turned The Tables On Me' is one of those swing-era tunes (recorded in 1937 by Benny Goodman) that never quite became a standard but thanks to Granz's beady eye was saved from obscurity by versions like this. Featuring a striking restrained solo from Oscar Peterson ('I was worried about being extra busy,' Peterson remembered, 'something I've always been charged with'), this cut is the highlight of the session.

Shavers put his mute in for 'Easy To Love', playing beautifully, Peterson takes the final cadence well away from the home key and Billie is heard to be making decisions not to go for Cole Porter's larger intervals ('…it does seem a shame') for sound aesthetic, not to say technical reasons. Billie's readings of 'These Foolish Things' and 'Solitude' display her in total control of her jazz and emotional instincts, while the brightest cut of the session, 'I Only Have Eyes For You', works fine until Billie's spontaneous interjection of 'big bulging eyes' in the coda, which unwarrantedly recalls the harrowing image in 'Strange Fruit'. Didn't she realise she could never refer to 'bulging eyes' in a romantic context ever again?

This session from late spring 1952 is also available on Billie Holiday: Solitude (Verve 519 810-2).

Disc 2
Los Angeles Studio Session (1952)

Everything I Have Is Yours/Love For Sale/
Moonglow/Tenderly/If The Moon Turns Green/
Remember/Autumn In New York (2 takes)

New York Studio Session (1952)

My Man/Lover Come Back To Me/Stormy Weather/
Yesterdays/He's Funny That Way/I Can't Face The
Music

*The first Granz session was amazingly productive (eight
sides, all issued) and the same team were clearly
inspired enough to reconvene a few days later for more
of the same. It is a treat to hear Billie sing the marvellous 1933 Burton Lane and Harold Adamson song
'Everything I Have Is Yours' (albeit a tad croakily) and
swing Irving Berlin's 1925 waltz 'Remember'. Another
swing-era staple, 'Moonglow', is convincingly recom-
posed, while 'When The Moon Turns Green' (written by
old pal Bernie Hanighen) is a rare example of Billie
recording a minor obscurity during the Granz sessions.
The presence of two rangy, awkward-to-sing songs of
quality ('Tenderly' and 'Autumn In New York') suggest
that Granz got more of his own way this time as far as
repertoire was concerned. (Consistent in what he wanted to hear these jazz singers sing, Granz had Ella
Fitzgerald and Louis Armstrong sing many of these same
songs on their duet albums of a few years later.)*

The diamond of this session, however, is a piano and

voice reading of Cole Porter's 'Love For Sale'. More than qualified than most to invest this candid, unsentimental song from a prostitute's viewpoint with some meaning, Billie's tired-eyed delivery brings vivid and unsettling irony to the already queasy lines 'Love that's fresh and still unspoiled/Love that's only slightly soiled'. Peterson is both prudently supportive and quietly inventive (on a chord sequence he doesn't sound completely comfortable with) in what is clearly an entirely spontaneous performance. '[Norman] wanted to display the complete interplay between us, and he wanted her to express the song anyway she felt,' said Peterson. 'He told me "Just go with her" – and so I did.'

This second session from late spring 1952 is also available on Billie Holiday: Solitude (Verve 519 810-2).

Back in New York, a 27 July 1952 session – billed as being by Billie Holiday and Her Lads Of Joy – sees the happy addition of contemporary Basie men to the group, including old flame Freddie Green (by now dubbed the greatest rhythm guitarist in the world), Joe Newman on trumpet and another beau of Billie's on tenor, Paul Quinichette (nick-named the 'Vice Pres' due to his similarity to Lester Young's playing style). A routine remake of 'My Man' adds nothing to her 1948 version, though a speedy 'Lover Come Back To Me' (featuring a glittering Peterson solo, one of the few times he got to stretch a little on a Holiday session) displays Billie having even more poise than on her 1944 version for Commodore.

As the most famous torch song of all, it is surprising that Billie had never before recorded 'Stormy Weather', but she presents it here like she's been singing it her whole life. Harolds Arlen's bluesy phrases sit so *comfortably in Billie's sound, she effortlessly banishes memories of Ethel Waters and Lena Horne by making it sound like it was written for her, acquiring it as her own forever.*

'Yesterdays' retains the dual tempo template of the 1939 Commodore version and displays similar horizontal melodic condensation from Billie, but her commanding delivery, her extraordinary melodic choices at the close (a D and held E, the 6th and #7th on F minor that becomes a #11th on Bb7) and Oscar's atmospheric organ chords mark it as the superior reading. A third studio remake of 'He's Funny That Way' boasts the charming and rare verse and remarkably fresh-sounding performance from Billie, while the lovely obscurity of the session is the underexposed 'Stormy Weather'-esque 'I Can't Face The Music' (same lyricist – Ted Koehler) with Billie in wonderful melodious mood, exercising excellent control of detailed nuance.

This 27 July 1952 session is also available in Recital By Billie Holiday *(Verve 521868-2).*

These initial sessions for Norman Granz were enthusiastically received in both Down Beat *(who gave* Billie Holiday Sings, *the first release, a five-star review) and* Metronome *(who asked 'Who can make familiar phrases of love requited, torches carried bravely and put down sadly, of passion so touching as Lady does?') though* Down Beat *recognised that Granz was not always winning the repertoire war: 'There are so many great tunes she hasn't recorded, she should stop inviting comparisons.'*

Disc 3
Jazz Club USA Concert – Germany (1954)

Blue Moon/All Of Me/My Man/Them There Eyes/I Cried For You/What A Little Moonlight Can Do/I Cover The Waterfront/Billie's Blues/Lover Come Back To Me

Following the opening flurry of sessions, Billie did not return to the studio for nearly two years, having to travel the country for her club work and further getting a reputation as a performer of unreliable quality. Reports included press comments varying from 'less than perfect' to 'by far the most impressive performer on the night', while Dan Morgenstern saw her in Boston in 1953 and thought she was in 'wonderful form'. Her fame as a notorious liver of life was consolidated by her appearance in the Comeback *TV show in October 1953, and in January 1954 she went to Europe as part of Leonard Feather's 'Jazz Club USA' tour.*

After a disastrous opening show in Stockholm on 12 January (following a nightmare journey and musicians, wary of her reputation, rowing and trying to avoid backing Billie's set), the tour settled down into a series of warm receptions for a much-loved jazz legend. By the time the tour arrived in Cologne on 23 January 1954, it was a happy and relaxed Billie who was recorded singing for the German audience.

It was not the most adventurous set (only 'Blue Moon' originates from her Granz-produced sessions) but that was hardly the point. 'All Of Me' and 'Them There Eyes' are strong, efficient and over in a blink. The inevitable 'My Man' is stalwartly performed in full voice (and featuring

a single, pointedly re-harmonised chord from pianist Carl Drinkard, plus an interestingly irreverent ending proving that even Billie's customised torchy moments could have their light touches). Almost twenty years after the first recording of 'What A Little Moonlight Can Do', she's still delivering a superbly swinging minimalist version, with Drinkard getting into the spirit with some bop substitution and Billie sounding cooler than ever.

The Cologne audience is treated to a sumptuous version of 'I Cover The Waterfront' (complete with moody verse à la the 1941 Okeh recording) and in the second set, sprawling jam-session treatments of 'Billie's Blues' and 'Lover Come Back To Me' with Billie's energy and charisma shining through the unkempt free-for-all.

New York Studio Session (1954)

How Deep Is The Ocean/What A Little Moonlight Can Do/I Cried For You

Perhaps inspired by the excitement generated by her recent live performances of oldies 'What A Little Moonlight Can Do' and 'I Cried For You' (a tune she referred to as 'my damn meat'), Billie decided to remake them in the studio on 14 April 1954 with the current Oscar Peterson trio (Ray Brown – bass, Herb Ellis – guitar) plus Ed Shaughnessy on drums and Charlie Shavers back on trumpet. 'Cried' is relatively routine, while 'Moonlight' is taken at a sizzling tempo and Billie, wisely avoiding those tricky downward intervallic leaps (which she never really made, even in the 1930s) gives one of her great performances, masterfully manoeuvring the rhythm of her lines, displaying undiminished expertise in what Oscar called 'the liberties she took with time'.

Irving Berlin's 'How Deep Is The Ocean' is the only fresh tune on the date and Billie makes fine, light work of it over a medium-brisk swinging groove. However, after only three sides were cut Granz shut down the session early with later recriminations flying from both band and singer. Peterson remembers the 'music going down the bottle', referring to what Billie was drinking ('things could only have gotten worse') while Billie blamed the band for turning up tired and drunk after flying in from a JATP tour. This tension is not remotely evident on the recorded musical legacy of the session.

This 14 April 1954 session is also available on Recital By Billie Holiday *(Verve 521868-2).*

Los Angeles Studio Session (1954)

Love Me Or Leave Me/PS I Love You/Too Marvelous For Words/Softly/I Thought About You/Willow Weep For Me/Stormy Blues

A 3 September 1954 date at Capitol Studios, Los Angeles produced seven sides featuring an entirely new (save the re-imported Barney Kessel on guitar) set of musicians. Harry 'Sweets' Edison and Willie Smith take the respective trumpet and alto obligatos (there are no solos) while Billie's old accompanist from the 1940s and faithful friend Bobby Tucker is on piano, with Red Callender (bass) and Chico Hamilton (drums) completing the rhythm section.

A faint glamourising sheen of echo on the sound (Granz's productions of the period were usually resolutely 'dry') only serve to point up the increasing rasp in Billie's sound, which is rather hard to swallow on the cosy domestic detail of a laughably unsuitable 'PS I Love You'; 'Write to the Browns just as soon as you're able/They came around to call'. However, her voice passes the swing test of 'Love Me Or Leave Me' and 'Too Marvelous For Words' and works wonderfully on the low-down bluesy pieces like 'Willow Weep For Me' and 'Stormy Blues'. The guttural chafe in her sound even gives delicate melodies like 'I Thought About You' a compellingly gruff, confessional edge and 'Softly' a husky, erotic quality.

This 3 September 1954 session is also available on Recital By Billie Holiday *(Verve 521868-2).*

New York Studio Session (1955)

Say It Isn't So/I've Got My Love To Keep Me Warm/ I Wished On The Moon/Always/Everything Happens To Me/Do Nothing Till You Hear From Me/Ain't Misbehavin'

Another seven sides resulted from the New York date on 14 February 1955, with Billie in tough form, negotiating the melodic detail in 'I've Got My Love To Keep Me Warm' with panache and nonchalantly recomposing 'Say It Isn't So'. Compared to the 1952 sides with Peterson, the group is relatively prosaic, with the rhythm section (featuring Cozy Cole who played drums on many of Billie's 1930s sides) decidedly pedestrian. A worthwhile revisit to 'I Wished On The Moon' – her first side on the Teddy Wilson date twenty years earlier – is preceded by a charming recitation of the rarely heard verse though the tentative soloists (Billy Bauer on guitar and, oddly, Shavers on trumpet) drag it down. Another Berlin waltz – 'Always' – is put into serviceable swing time with tenorist Budd Johnson delivering a generic solo through Tony Scott's garrulous, modernist clarinet tussles with Cole's straight-backed work all the way.

Matt Dennis's 'Everything Happens To Me' is a good example of a previously unrecorded song that fits Lady like a glove as she brings an attractive blend of resignation and humour to the fatalist lyric. Likewise, Ellington's 'Do Nothing Till You Hear From Me' is perfect for her – just by engaging with it here ranks it among Billie's most essential cuts – and while she appears to stroll through 'Ain't Misbehavin'', even a casual Holiday performance of a song that becomes her is enough to wrench it from the comic clutches of its composer Fats Waller.

This 4 February 1955 session can also be found on Lady Sings The Blues (Verve 521429-2).

Disc 4
Rehearsal At Artie Shapiro's Home (1955)
– Includes Studio Discussion

Nice Work If You Can Get It/Mandy Is Two/Prelude To A Kiss/I Must Have That Man/Jeepers Creepers/Please Don't Talk About Me When I'm Gone/Moonlight In Vermont/Misery/Restless/Everything Happens To Me/I Don't Want To Cry Anymore/When You Are Away Dear/It Had To Be You/The Mood That I'm In/Gone With The Wind/

I Got It Bad And That Ain't Good/A Sunbonnet Blue/ Ghost Of A Chance/I'm Walkin' Through Heaven With You/Just Friends/The Nearness Of You/It's Too Hot For Words/They Say/I Won't Believe It

On Monday 22 August 1955, Billie gathered with pianist Jimmy Rowles at bassist Artie Shapiro's house in Los Angeles to prepare for a recording session (which didn't involve Shapiro) scheduled for the following day. It was Rowles's idea to rehearse, not being so convinced that Granz's last-minute spontaneity always produced the best recorded results, particularly when dealing with the standard of tune that was favoured. 'We never had time to get together on chords, Barney Kessle, the bassist and me,' remembered Rowles. 'Now that's really difficult, especially when Norman would pull out a tune and say: "Here it is: 'Prelude To A Kiss'… go!" Everyone's got their own conception of how to play the tune and so it comes out sounding like a jam session.' Unbeknown to Billie and Rowles, Shapiro taped the rehearsal.

In 1973 a forty-five minute LP was released of the rehearsal but the Complete Verve *set has restored it to a seventy-nine minute session. 'I've only listened to that rehearsal tape once,' said Rowles. 'I was disgusted that it was released because Billie was pretty loaded and it seemed like I was trying to catch up with her. She had gone through a whole pint of vodka before I could get her dressed, and that she was when I woke her up at noon'.*

Understandable as Rowle's unhappiness with its avail-ability is, for those interested in Billie Holiday's art and personality (loaded or not), it is a fascinating glimpse

into her world and working process. Gravel-voiced and a shade confused here and there, Billie nevertheless puts in some rigorous preparation time on keys, tempos, grooves and endings by simply singing what she wants and expecting Rowles (as he suggests in his comment) to 'catch up with her'.

With Billie growling assertively through the melody to 'Nice Work If You Can Get It', Rowles splashes around the piano in Db trying to find the chord changes to the bridge before admonishing her: 'You goddamn bitch, you've come up with the god-awfulest key in life'. She sings a good coda and then promptly forgets it so Rowles reminds her and she asks him to write it out. 'I won't remember it tomorrow. See, I'll be in a different mood…I don't always feel the same. I just can't do it. I can't even copy me [laughs]. I've tried.'

They mess around a little with 'Mandy Is Two' (one of the last Columbia sides and one of Billie's great sentimental moments) with Rowles grunting his obvious approval as Billie unfolds the affecting melody for him as he attempts to pick it out. A complete run-through performance (with no asides or instructions) of 'A Prelude To A Kiss' with an intimately-recorded Billie vocal suggests that perhaps by this time she was aware that the rehearsal was being taped.

One of the revelatory aspects of this rehearsal tape is the insight into Billie's way with time that was such a source of wonder to Oscar Peterson. Though Peterson exaggeratedly observed, 'Billie wasn't even aware that there were four beats going on behind her,' he must have been aware that her over-the-beat phrasing was hardly luck, and these tapes are a rare example of the Holiday rhythm machine in all its glory.

In the absence of a drummer or bassist (Shapiro most-
ly sits out), Billie conveys her tempo preferences with the
brightest, tightest finger popping imaginable, while all
the time uninhibitedly phrasing on, off and around the
beat in her usual fashion. Here she is the unassailable
source of the ground beat and the untethered song stylist operating all at the same time. 'Jeepers Creepers' and
'Please Don't Talk About Me When I'm Gone' swing better and deeper with just her popping and clapping along
with Rowles than with some of the rhythm sections she
worked with. ('Yeah, yeah, yeah, that's a bitch!' enthuses
Rowles.) And when she wants to change the feel of a
tune (like 'Everything Happens To Me' and 'I Don't Want
To Cry Anymore': 'I want that son-of-a-bitch jumpin',
because you know everybody else would make it pretty'), she does so with a marvellously expressive shift in
her depiction of the time (and some economic, animat-
ed expletives) and there's no mistaking what she
means.

Billie indulges in some goading reminiscences about
the first meeting with Rowles in 1942 and he distract-
edly tinkers at the piano. They talk about her dog, Pepi.
Billie wants to teach Rowles 'Misery', Tony Scott's song
('I've been promising that boy now for years') but, unwill-
ing to pick it out without a lead sheet, Rowles distracts
her by trying to teach her 'Restless' (and later the equally obscure 'When You Are Away Dear'), and we can hear
her alert vocal reactions to Rowles's clear melody leading at the piano, though it goes no further than an initial run-through.

Billie pitches 'Moonlight In Vermont' in another tricky
key. 'You sing in Gb all the time,' observes Rowles. 'It's a
beautiful key. I wish I'd been playin' it in the last year'.

Billie instantly takes on board Rowles's suggestion of a hip chromatic variation on the melody to 'Everything Happens To Me', but they lose their way somewhat during an extended work out of 'I Don't Want To Cry Any More'. Other tunes given cursory attention (but not developed in the studio) include 'They Say' (recorded for Columbia in 1938), 'I'm Walking Through Heaven With You' (never recorded) and the modern jazz staple 'Just Friends' (also never recorded).

It is here that Billie is heard complaining about the aborted 14 April 1954 date, where only three sides were recorded (though she confuses the personnel) and recalls her audition at Ed Small's where she didn't know what key she sang anything in. She also muses on 'me and my old voice. It just go up a little bit and come down a little bit. It's not legit.' It is these kind of asides that give the rehearsal tapes of 22 August 1955 such a unique, immediate sense of Billie Holiday's complex presence. Drunk, provocative (she teases Rowles about not leading the rehearsal more assertively), full of memories, bitchy, vulnerable, rhythmically astounding, vocally limited; being able to eavesdrop on all this is a quietly overwhelming experience.

Disc 5
Los Angeles Studio Session (1955)
– Includes Studio discussion

I Don't Want To Cry Anymore (2 takes)/Prelude To A Kiss (2 takes)/Ghost Of A Chance/When Your Lover Has gone (3 takes)/Gone With The Wind/Please Don't Talk About Me When I'm Gone/It Had To Be You/Nice Work If You Can Get It/Come Rain Or Shine/I Got A Right To Sing The Blues/What's New/A Fine Romance (8 takes)/I Hadn't Any One Till You

Disc 6
Los Angeles Studio Session (1955)

I Get A Kick Out Of You/Everything I Have Is Yours/Isn't This A Lovely Day

The session the Rowles rehearsal was leading to on 23 August was an extensive one split into two. Billie was impressed with Granz's instruction to 'sing as long as I can hold out' and though she didn't manage the eighteen sides Art Tatum had knocked off on his recent session, the eight sides achieved was productive by vocal standards.

Happily, the band is of a high standard, featuring old pal Benny Carter as ostensible leader plus Kessel, Edison, Rowles, John Simmons on bass and Larry Bunker on drums. This session concentrated on unrecorded superior ballads of the romantic – 'It Had To Be You', 'Prelude To A Kiss' – but more often of the regretful and lovelorn type; 'I Don't Want To Cry Any More', 'A Ghost

Of A Chance', 'When Your Lover Has Gone', 'Gone With The Wind'.

While sometimes exposing the technical limitations of Billie's voice, these performances are full of subtle nuances of interpretation that reward a sympathetic listen. It is interesting that for all her continued rhythmic authority on brighter tempos (marvellously displayed on a boisterous 'Please Don't Talk About Me When I'm Gone' and a creamily swinging 'Nice Work If You can Get It', that Billie (and, presumably, Norman Granz) felt continuously drawn to the slower tempos with their exposing melodies and textures.

Two days later on 25 August 1955 Billie was back in the studio with the same band and in discernably better voice on six new tunes ('Come Rain Or Come Shine', 'What's New?', 'I Hadn't Anyone Till You', 'I Get A Kick Out Of You', 'Everything I Have Is Yours', 'Isn't This A Lovely Day?') and two re-makes ('I Got A Right To Sing The Blues' and 'A Fine Romance').

Despite some dreary tempos and an awkward foray into a beguine groove for 'Kick', the ballads are interestingly chosen, though again she fares better on the bluer tunes, once more showing her affinity with Harold Arlen on his 'Come Rain' and a gritty remake of 'I Got A Right'. 'Romance' shows great rhythmic flexibility and humour as she grapples with three of Dorothy Fields's clever, wordy stanzas, though this sort of arch wit wasn't really her forte. Rowles and Carter are inventive and supportive throughout.

These sessions of 23 and 25 August 1955 are also available on Music For Torching (Verve 527455-2).

Rehearsal At The Duftys' Home (1956)

Misery/Israel/I Must Have That Man/Strange Fruit/
God Bless The Child/One Never Knows – Does
One?/Beer Barrel Polka/Some Of These Days/A
Yiddishe Momma/Lady's Back In Town

*On 30 May 1956 Billie joined clarinettist-pianist Tony
Scott at William and Maely Duftys' home to rehearse
for the album* Lady Sings The Blues, *which was con-
ceived to tie in with the forthcoming William Dufty-
penned autobiography and for which Scott was the MD.
The tape is valuable for Billie's only known recording of
Scott's moody, minor-key piece 'Misery' that he had composed for her seven years earlier (and that she had told
Jimmy Rowles on the earlier rehearsal tape she felt bad
about not getting round to). Scott, meanwhile, had let
Carmen McRae record it on her first album. 'I shouldn't
be speaking to you Tony, you know that,' teases Billie.
'Don't speak to me then,' retorts Scott, 'I shouldn't be
speaking to you. It's seven years ago [laughter].'*

*Once more, Billie appears in a confused state and while
trying to sing 'I Must Have That Man' is unable to extri-
cate its lyrics from the melody of 'He's Funny That Way'.
While sharing similar metric shapes, they are distinctive
enough songs not to be confused normally, though Scott
continuing to play the chords of the latter is obviously not
helping Billie to think clearly. Compared to the intensive
quality of the Rowles rehearsal, this is relatively leisurely
and is mainly taken up with the rowdy entertainment of
the Duftys' fifteen-month-old son, Bevan. It is only marginally more interesting than listening to any home recordings
of people you don't know.*

New York Studio Session (1956)

Trav'lin' Light/I Must Have That Man/Some Other
Spring/Lady Sings The Blues/Strange Fruit/God Bless
The Child/Good Morning Heartache/No Good
Man

Los Angeles Studio Session (1956)

Do Nothing Till You Hear From Me/Cheek To
Cheek/Ill Wind/Speak Low/We'll Be Together
Again/All Or Nothing At All/Sophisticated
Lady/April In Paris

By its nature, the Lady Sings The Blues *recording project was to feature a retrospective song list, particularly
those pieces which had (or could be interpreted as having) personal significance to Billie. Though the septet of
musicians gathered to remake the songs on 6 and 7
June 1956 was an intriguing blend of generations and
styles (including twenty-four-year-olds Wynton Kelly on
piano and Kenny Burrell on guitar, thirty-three-year-old
Scott, forty-year-old Paul Quinichette on tenor and forty-
eight-year-old Charlie Shavers) it never really gels. Scott's
arrangements are perfunctory (mainly intros and outros)
and rather quaint, with neither the splendour of her
best-arranged sessions nor the fizz of her best spontaneous dates (though Shavers's seemingly inappropriate,
triumphant fanfares at the top of 'Strange Fruit' and
'Lady Sings The Blues' are peculiarly arresting). The lack
of attention to authentic detail is exemplified by Scott
and Holiday recording their befuddled 'I Must Have That*

Man'/'He's Funny That Way' hybrid, titling it as the for-mer, thereby confusing many listeners (unfamiliar with Billie's 1937 classic reading of 'Man') for years.

No one is allowed to solo so the obbligatos are care-fully, self-consciously distributed, with Lady singing her chestnuts ('Good Morning Heartache', 'God Bless The Child', 'Strange Fruit') reasonably well, but without any particular spark of inspiration. The best cuts are a wel-come return to 'Some Other Spring' (though it doesn't trouble the 1939 version), 'No Good Man' (one of Billie's customised Mean Daddy songs from the Decca years) and a new Holiday original, co-written with pianist Herbie Nichols, 'Lady Sings The Blues'. It is an ungainly composition but it does have some low-down spirit and it is something new for Lady to get her teeth into.

The sessions of 6 and 7 June 1955 are also available on Lady Sings The Blues (Verve 521429-2).

Back with Messrs Rowles, Kessel and Edison along with old musician pal and flame Ben Webster on deeply empathetic tenor saxophone, the 14 and 18 August 1956 sessions were more like it. Billie is perhaps at her most fragile, vocally, on this date and yet, as always, she makes the best of what she has and there are things to enjoy on all eight sides.

All new, high-quality songs (except the year-on remake of 'Do Nothing Till You Hear From Me'), Harold Arlen's 'Ill Wind' is perfect for her and despite the most diminished sound yet heard from Lady, with the help of ultra-sensi-tive backing from Kessel, a sumptuous solo from Webster along with the tailor-made material, something memo-rable and moving occurs. She cannot quite reinvent Berlin's 'Cheek To Cheek' quickly enough to disguise her inability to make the top-to-bottom nature of the melody, *but she stays rhythmically perky throughout. She floats 'Speak Low' unconcernedly over the band's attempt at a Latin groove, swings the difficult 'All Or Nothing At All' with authority, makes the most of the considerable requirements of 'Sophisticated Lady' and fashions something gnarled but elegant from 'April In Paris'.*

These sessions of 14 and 18 August 1956 are also available on All Or Nothing At All *(Verve 529226-2).*

Disc 8
Carnegie Hall Concert (1956) – Includes readings from the book Lady Sings The Blues

Lady Sings The Blues/Ain't Nobody's Business If I Do/Trav'lin' Light/Billie's Blues/Body And Soul/Don't Explain/Yesterdays/Please Don't Talk About Me When I'm Gone/I'll Be Seeing You/My Man/I Cried For You/Fine And Mellow/I Cover The Waterfront

On 10 November 1956, Billie Holiday gave two shows – at 8pm and midnight – incorporating songs strongly associated with her and her life along with, in case the point was missed, readings from her recently published, sensational 'autobiography' Lady Sings The Blues. New York Times *columnist Gilbert Millstein was drafted in to intone Duftys' prose at four points in the concert and what could have been a mawkish celebration of painful struggle accompanied by faded-but-forgivable performances turned into triumph.*

The concert took on the vivid impact of a theatrical performance, with Millstein's voice bringing a solemn nobility to the atmosphere and Billie rising to the event

with palpable spirit. Her first musical entrance following Millstein's opening reading is spine-chilling. It is partly timing – she picks up her cue with the precision of a film edit – and partly the dignified wail in her sound as she sings 'La-a-dy sings the blues…' with a magnificent sense of occasion. 'The context in which she sang,' wrote Nat Hentoff in Down Beat, *'was the most extraordinary this reviewer had ever encountered in a concert hall'.*

In these surroundings the song 'Lady Sings The Blues' is transformed from the amorphous and uncertain studio reading of five months earlier into a vibrantly alive personal statement; it is hard not to hear the warm applause that greets the closing lines 'Now the world will know/She's never gonna sing 'em no more/No more' as tantamount to a flood of relief that Lady isn't going to die before our very eyes, not tonight.

Millstein reads about Billie leaving Baltimore and Lady and the band quietly play 'Trav'lin' Light' behind him, Millstein reads the lipstick-on-Jimmy-Monroe's-collar story and Billie sings 'Don't Explain', Millstein reads the final lines of the book: 'Tired? You bet. But all that I'll soon forget with my man…' and Billie sings 'My Man'. It works brilliantly.

The band included regular and improved accompanist Carl Drinkard – with Roy Eldridge (trumpet) and Coleman Hawkins (tenor) in the first set, Buck Clayton (trumpet), Tony Scott (clarinet) and Al Cohn (tenor) in the second – and were discreet and exemplary, limited as they were to obbligatos. The audience were delirious, demanding numerous encores, even the musicians applauded her and Hentoff wrote, unequivocally, that Billie was 'undeniably the best and most honest jazz singer alive'.

This concert recording of 10 November 1956 is also available on At Carnegie Hall *(Verve 527777-2).*

Disc 9
Los Angeles Studio Sessions (1957)
– Includes Studio Talk

I Wished On The Moon/Moonlight In Vermont/ A Foggy Day/I Didn't Know What Time It Was/ Just One Of Those Things (2 takes)/Comes Love (4 takes)

Los Angeles Studio Sessions (1957)
– Includes Studio Talk

Day In Day Out/Darn That Dream/But Not For Me/Body And Soul/Just Friends (instrumental)/Stars Fell On Alabama (2 takes)/Say It Isn't So (2 takes)/Our Love Is Here To Stay (2 takes)/One For My Baby (And One More For The Road) (3 takes)/ They Can't Take That Away From Me/Embraceable You/Let's Call The Whole Thing Off/Gee Baby Ain't I Good To You

In January 1957 Billie was back in LA with her favourite West Coast recording unit (Rowles, Edison, Webster, Kessel, plus Red Mitchell on bass and Alvin Stoller on drums) for a marathon eighteen sides recorded at five sessions. Once more, this group proves that they were perhaps the most supportive, sympathetic jazz accompanists Billie had in her final decade. The solos from Webster are never less than mouth-watering, Edison's muted contributions always pert and tactful, Kessel is swinging and resourceful, Rowles quirky and sensitive.

Billie's frailty on the sessions of 3 and 4 January is further exposed in Verve's ever-clear recording quality. A tiny cracking sound and erratic pitching on some Granz-nominated quality-but-tricky tunes at determinedly revealing tempos ('Moonlight In Vermont', 'I Didn't Know What Time It Was') will never endear these performances to lovers of pure vocal tone. But once more, her timing and shading with an upbeat or ironic lyric make 'Just One Of Those Things' and 'Comes Love' valuable sides.

A few days' break and Billie is on fine form for the 7 January session, with all the sides having something to commend them. By now Granz is letting the band relax and stretch with three of the four sides nearing the six-and-a-half-minute mark, everyone taking some solo space. These sides present Billie being back as one of the boys in the band and it becomes her.

The perfectly tempoed 'Day In Day Out' and 'But Not For Me' are relaxed and delightful and Billie meets the challenge of Jimmy Van Heusen's labyrinthine melody for 'Darn That Dream' with grace and skill. 'Body And Soul', though it appears on occasional live recordings, had not been examined in the studio since 1940, and the intervening years have brought a wealth of nuance to her reading.

Billie was late to the session of the following day on 8 January 1957 but still salvaged four precious sides. 'Stars Fell On Alabama' and 'Our Love Is Here To Stay' are the kind of comfortable mid-tempo performances that showed everyone off in a satisfying light.

'Say It Isn't So' is set in suitably defeated tones (and much more engaging than the 1955 side with Tony Scott) while 'One For My Baby (And One More For The

Road)' though written for a 1941 Fred Astaire movie, is another Harold Arlen piece that sounds like it was written for her. Billie's reading of it is entirely different to Frank Sinatra's romantic-tragic classic he recorded a year or so later, but in its world-weary bluesy groove and the undeniable authenticity in Billie's barfly delivery, it is a contender for the definitive version and a sort of apex of her final few years' music. In a way, she always sounded like she was singing 'One For My Baby'.

The following day's work on 9 January 1957 was perhaps even more rewarding. Two Gershwin tunes ('They Can't Take That Away From Me' and 'Let's Call The Whole Thing Off') are dispatched with such appropriate verve, it is regretful that more of her Verve recordings were not along these lines. The extended, tender reading of a third Gershwin, however – 'Embraceable You' – is also sufficiently gratifying to suggest that Billie was just in good form generally.

Yet the jewel, as it so often was in this period, is the lowdown, bluesy groover, in this case 'Gee Baby Ain't I Good To You?', which although heard at her 1946 JATP recording, had never been attempted in the studio before. Her final chorus – her third, full of muscular, high variations – is so strong, it can't help but temporarily and speciously encourage the listener that all is well and all would be well.

The sessions of January 1957 are also available on All Or Nothing At All (Verve 529226-2).

Disc 10
Newport Jazz Festival (1957)

Nice Work If You Can Get It/Willow Weep For Me/My Man/Lover Come Back To Me/Lady Sings

The Blues/What A Little Moonlight Can Do

In May 1957, Norman Granz made it known he would not be renewing Billie's contract with Verve Records. He had eventually managed to sign Ella Fitzgerald to his company the previous year and was finding it infinitely easier to pursue extensive, reliable, jazz-inflected recordings of his Great American Songbook with Ella than he ever could with Billie. On 6 July 1957, Billie appeared at the Newport Jazz Festival in delicate shape and sounded tired but still fighting; down but not yet out.

Her version of 'My Man' has aching pauses between phrases in the verse creating a real drama and she negotiates the speedier tunes with customary casualness. However, as her final recording to appear on Verve, it was originally issued along with Ella Fitzgerald's set at the same festival and it makes for a cruelly telling comparison. Ella had been Billie's contemporary since the mid-1930s and between them they represented the double apex of female jazz singing, but Ella had consistently been more professional, more popular and, importantly, healthier and here it was to be heard; two stars passing each other on the stage, one rising the other falling.

The 1957 Newport set is also available on Billie Holiday: Jazz At The Philharmonic *(Verve 521642-2).*

Seven Ages Of Jazz Concert (1958)

I Wished On The Moon/Lover Man

These two sides recorded at a 26 September 1958 Leonard Feather promotion find Billie in as good a form as she'd been in the previous six years. 'I Wished On The Moon' is rhythmically intrepid and 'Lover Man' has an emotional and musical focus that some of her ballad performances of this period missed. That it is so much more convincing than the 1957 Newport set proves that the below-par performances at this time in her life were not necessarily ubiquitous. The relieved, roaring calls for an encore attest to the anxiety in the audience that must have anticipated Lady's appearances in late 1958.

New York Studio Session (1959)

All The Way/It's Not For Me To Say/I'll Never Smile Again/Just One More Chance/When It's Sleepy Time Down South/Don't Worry 'Bout Me/Sometimes I'm Happy/You Took Advantage Of Me/There'll Be Some Changes Made/'Deed I Do/All Of You/Baby Won't You Please Come Home?

Originally released on MGM which is now part of the Polygram/Universal group and is therefore eligible for the Verve Box, the 1959 New York studio session was recorded after Lady In Satin *(see below), so for the purposes of this discography appears non-chronologically as part of Disc 10 of* The Complete Billie Holiday on Verve.

Sufficiently encouraged by Lady In Satin, *which had been recorded a year earlier, Billie signed with MGM and recorded twelve more sides with Ray Ellis in March 1959. Though the choir was eliminated and the strings were dampened, just saving some of these sides from being* Lady In Satin II, *for many listeners – in all its* palpable weakness and qualified strengths – it will be a comparable experience. Desperately weak, Billie had to be held on a stool by nurse Alice Vrbsky to sing at the session. Surprisingly, the vocal results are not quite as feeble as one might expect. The note-to-rasp ratio is healthier than on Lady In Satin, with the same melodies to an interesting set of songs including 'I'll Never Smile Again', 'When It's Sleepy Time Down South' and 'Don't Worry 'Bout Me' are dependably and sensitively picked out. There are even a few serviceable medium swingers: 'Sometimes I'm Happy', featuring some nifty alto work from Gebe Guill, and 'Deed I Do' featuring some risky, successful re-working from Billie. The album ends with an intriguingly vivid version of 'Baby Won't You Please Come Home', beginning with a breezily delivered chorus before reprising the entire song in pleading half-time phrases. Though many will argue with Down Beat's generous assertion in reviewing the posthumously released album that 'in spite of everything, Lady Day had it right up to the end' (Will Friedwald more realistically characterises the hopeful signs as 'flowers sprouting in a graveyard'), Billie's final musical statement contains a quality that her penultimate record perhaps lacked – dignity.

These March 1959 sessions are also available on Billie Holiday Last Recordings (Verve 835370-2).

Lady In Satin

(Columbia CK 65144)

I'm a Fool To Want You/For Heavens Sake/You Don't Know What Love Is/I Get Along Without You

Very Well/For All We Know/Violets For Your Furs/
You've Changed/It's Easy To Remember/But
Beautiful/Glad To Be Unhappy/I'll Be Around/End
Of A Love Affair

*These were the first sessions recorded with Ray Ellis. For
all* Lady In Satin's *controversy, the album has remained
in the shops in one form or another more consistently
than any of her other sessions, continues to sell and will
divide the room for as long as people still listen to it.
Being such a subjective experience,* Lady In Satin *is
almost beyond the reach of dispassionate critical comment. Technical vocal difficulties aside, some of it is
indeed pitiful — Billie clearly just does not know 'Glad To
Be Unhappy' or 'I'll Be Around' well enough (didn't she
have Sinatra's* In The Wee Small Hours *album?) —
though her last minute reading of 'You've Changed' (a
song short, Billie and Ellis popped out to a music shop
to pick the tune together) ranks with any Holiday ballad
performance since 1952.*

*Ellis's work has a certain old-fashioned allure and does
the prescribed job well enough, while the occasional
majestic trombone contribution from JJ Johnson arrives
at the listener like the welcome reminder of a life force.
As for the sorry state of Billie's voice, the ear has a way
of adjusting to begin to hear beyond tonal shortcomings
into the minutiae of phrasing, inevitably discerning
unavoidable poignancy in certain lines. Whether heart-
rending testament to the expressive spirit of a great
jazz artist or the sound of someone dying before our
very ears,* Lady In Satin *should be heard by anyone
interested in the story of Billie Holiday.*

THREE

CRITIQUE

Billie Holiday's achievements as a jazz musician are, these days, rather overpowered by the legend of her life and iconic status as mistress of misery. Leaving aside the obvious problems of the *Lady In Satin* period, when listeners actually hear her, even at her peak, they are often surprised at what they find. Of course, Billie's voice had some precedent in the blues moan of Bessie Smith and the musical invention of Louis Armstrong, and her influence on succeeding generations of popular singers can hardly be overestimated, yet the actual experience of *hearing* her sing is unique; the keening, floating sound – grainy and sassy yet with a melancholy centre; the rhythmic and melodic playfulness; the lyric timed with the instinct of a dramatic actress. Billie Holiday remains unlike any other encounter in music.

Hearing Ella Fitzgerald, one may be stuck by her purity of tone; hearing Sarah Vaughan, one may be impressed by her technical mastery and musical intelligence; but hearing Billie Holiday, the prime effect on most listeners is an emotional one. As contemporary singer-pianist Diana Krall has put it, 'She really makes you feel.' At her best moments, Billie Holiday had a way of reading a song that gives it an added dimension of resonance. And it wasn't just to do with connecting the life with the music; it was a combination of expressive diction, timbral gestures and nuances of timing that gave the impression less of a singer singing, but rather *inhabiting* the song. As jazz singer Sheila Jordan has said, 'She just had this way of being so damn personal, and I believed her.' To put it simply, Billie Holiday *acted* a song.

The impact of her more emotionally resounding performances, along with the concerted effort latterly in her career to establish an overt correspondence between material and performer (and Billie's widely quoted assertion that she can only sing what she 'feels') have led to a widely held view that, as friend, sometime maid, sometime songwriter, jazz singer Carmen McRae observes, 'she sang the way she was. That's really Lady when you listen to her on record.'

The quality, while sometimes producing vivid and compelling listening experiences, becomes problematic on two fronts. Firstly, how is a listener to respond to a song of blatant, unapologetic masochistic dependency like 'My Man'? Or a cheerfully defiant song of ill-advised loyalty like ''Tain't Nobody's Business If I Do'? Are we to nod with appreciation at her candid self-expression on receipt of lines like 'I promise I won't call no copper/When I get beat up by my Poppa'? In presenting herself and her values in contentious material like this so unflinchingly, she is defying the audience not to judge her while still expecting their patronage. Female subservience may not have been such an ideological problem in the 1940s and 1950s, but modern listeners have little option but to be discomforted.

Secondly, hearing Billie Holiday sing 'the way she was' when she was audibly suffering the fall-out of a life of self-abuse is a deeply unsettling experience. Here is a lady who, for whatever reasons (Stuart Nicholson suggests that she suffered from what would now be diagnosed as a psychopathic personality disorder) had indulged in excessive, life-long self-destructive habits, and we are compelled to listen to the results. *The Lady In Satin* period of the late 1950s is 'painful listening', admits bassist Milt Hinton, 'because it is the audio equivalent of shoving a video camera in the face of someone who is grieving'.

Some deal with this discomfort by simply avoiding it. Biographer, John Chilton: 'It is not squeamishness to prefer hearing Billie when she was able to give insight into a whole range of human emotions rather than listening to…the sounds of a sick woman in despair.' Pianist-songwriter and early Holiday fan Dave Frishberg declares: 'I don't even listen to it even though many musicians I respect rave about it…this aspect of Billie Holiday doesn't interest me, nor does it reach me.'

Yet, as Frishberg suggests, many rate *Lady In Satin* among Billie's greatest achievements. Drumming legend Max Roach – speaking for those that John Chilton calls the 'hear how she suffers' listeners – loves it because 'it told a lot about her life, her loves, her emotional ups and downs, what she had been through.' Composer and jazz cabaret artist Richard Rodney Bennet finds it 'so moving, the flaws, the vulnerability'. Jimmy Rowles was very protective of it, even getting angry if it was criticised.

This audaciously personal aspect to Billie Holiday's music means it is almost impossible for modern listeners to approach what Holiday achieved musically without getting involved with the story of her life and attempting an understanding of her character. It may be that the connections between Billie Holiday's art and her life are forever inextricable and perhaps, in this case, that is how it should be.

People who knew and worked with Billie, or who were attracted to her or got hooked on the vibrancy of her personality, naturally have the strongest emotional bond to her music. Leonard Feather speaks for many fans, friends and musicians of his generation when he writes touchingly of the connection felt with Billie by those who were there, growing up with her career and music. 'Perhaps the only thing you can do is take a backward journey through time and be born in the twenties, so that the arrival of Billie's glorious four years of regular sessions with the Teddy Wilson combos will coincide with your high school or college days. And by the time she spends a full year at the Onyx on Fifty-second Street, reducing audiences of noisy drunks to silence with her gracious, dignified, gardenia-embellished beauty as she sings her brand-new hit "Lover Man", you will be in your twenties, and part of a warm and wonderful new jazz era that is growing with Billie.'

As the decline sets in, Feather beautifully explains the position of the intimate fan. 'By the time you are in your thirties you will have been so conditioned to a love of the Holiday sound that you will excuse the little flaws, the gradual withdrawal of assurance, the fading of the gardenia. By now you are in love with Lady Day and everything she does; each tortured lyric she sings about men who have laid waste her life will have meaning for you whether she hits the note or misses it, holds it or lets it falter.'

Her in-person charisma as a performer and a personality meant that many friends and acquaintances were in thrall to her. British jazz writer Max Jones characterised her as 'bright, tough, realistic, stylish, transparently sincere most of the time, and lovable for much of it' during his chauffeuring and gofering of Billie on her visits to England, describing the experience as 'one of the most quietly spectacular achievements of my jazz-hacking years'. As Maele Dufty, friend and wife of Billie's biographer, observed, 'Billie's not a woman – she's a habit.'

Personal involvements aside, how do we assess just how good

Billie Holiday was? Down the years, many commentators less involved with her life and career have tried to measure what they were hearing on its own terms. It started with Apollo Theatre emcee and disc jockey Ralph Cooper attempting to describe Billie's singing by saying, 'It ain't the blues. I don't know what it is, but you got to hear her.'

John S Wilson of the *New York Times* later continued trying to clear up the difficulty of labelling exactly what 'kind' of singer Billie was. 'Unlike almost all those who are classified as jazz singers, Billie Holiday is basically neither a blues singer nor that type of singer of popular ballads who is identified as a "pop" singer. She draws from both sources but depends on neither. She is, purely and simply, a jazz singer.'

Founder of *Rolling Stone* and *San Francisco Chronicle* and *Down Beat* jazz critic Ralph J Gleason concurs, emphasising her pervading influence. 'She was a singer of jazz, the greatest female jazz voice of all time, a great interpreter, a great actress and the creator of a style that, in its own way, is as unique and important to jazz as the styles of Louis Armstrong, Charlie Parker and Lester Young...Today, if you sing jazz and you are a woman, you sing some of Billie Holiday. There is no other way to do it. No vocalist is without her influence. All girl singers sing some of Billie, like all trumpet players play some of Louis. She wrote the text.'

One of the characteristics associated with 'jazz' singing (as opposed to any other kind) is scat, i.e. improvised instrumental-type melodies sung with nonsense syllables; an effect that attempts to establish vocalists on an improvising par with instrumentalists. Billie Holiday never scatted. Her manipulations were always confined within the delivery of the lyric. As vocalese- and scat-meister Jon Hendricks observed, 'she was more interested in the emotion in the song rather than the structure of the chords on which the song is based, which is what you're interested in if you scat.'

Yet critiques of Holiday consistently allude to her instinctive, horn-like invention. Benny Green observes, 'to her, singing was not so much the exercise of an artistic function as the natural means of expression towards the world. This relationship involving the mechanics of making music is common enough among the best instrumentalists...The casual effects she threw off would be psychological masterstrokes had they been thought out and planned ahead. As it was, they remained emphatic triumphs of intuition.'

For those taking it to this level of appreciation, it is useful to examine one or two of Billie's 'triumphs of intuition', in relation to one of the striking aspects of her art, her horn-like recasting or recomposition of a melody. Generally, most composed (and improvised) melodic phrases come to rest on a strong chord tone, that is the root, 3rd, 5th or 7th of the prevailing chord. Broadly, the root and 3rd of the chord are considered the strongest, homeiest of the available notes, the 5th is also strong, if a little more remote, while the 7th is considered the more colourful of the chord tones.

Generally, untrained 'ear' musicians (of whom Billie Holiday was one) gravitate their improvisations safely to the root and 3rd notes of the chord (sometimes, even safer, the root and 3rd of the central key, as in Billie's 'I'll Get By' and 'Without Your Love') but Billie is willing to foray into the upper partials of chords – eg 9ths and 13ths – especially, interestingly, on blues material where melodic opportunities are not traditionally exploited. For example, on 'Long Gone Blues' (1939), her second phrase ('Tell me what's the matter now') settles on a C natural, the 9th of the Bb chord, while the first phrase of her second stanza ('I've been your slave') comes to rest on a G natural, the 6th (or 13th) note of the Bb chord. These are usually the note choices of certain composers and improvising melodic instrumentalists, whose ears are trained to pick out the 'pretty' notes, yet this is the creative level Billie worked at instinctively.

Billie's 'Georgia On My Mind' (1941) is perhaps one of the finest examples of her horn-like rearranging of a melody. A few examples: the composed opening notes ('Georgia...') are D–F, the 3rd–5th of the Bb major chord, Billie sings D–F–G, the 3rd–5th–6th. Already she hears and places colourful elements into the music that make it hers. The opening of the second stanza ('Georgia, Georgia...') should again be D–F (3rd–5th of Bb major) then D–C (Root–7th of D7 chord), an exotic enough move from the pen of jazz-drenched composer Hoagy Carmichael. Billie takes it several steps further by singing Bb–A (Root–7th of Bb major) the F#–E (3rd–9th of D7), an extraordinarily sophisticated substitution to have been heard, let alone sung with such insouciance. Even at this distance, educated by bebop and beyond as our ears are, the audacity of this tiny moment still has the power to thrill.

It is tempting to argue that by singing the floating 9th rather than the bluesy 7th on the second 'Georgia', she gives the yearning for the dear old South (!) a hesitant poignancy rather than a deep-felt longing; rather appropriate given how the South treated her when she was with Artie Shaw. However, while her note choices may well enhance 'the emotional impact of the lyric' as Green and others suggest, it is likely that often, like a horn player, she was just having a blow.

Although Billie's widely quoted defensive assertion when she was sacked by Basie's management ('I hate straight singing. I have to change a tune to my own way of doing it. That's all I know.') is often taken at face value and has been interpreted as the mission statement of a creative musician to 'improve' inferior material, that is clearly not the whole story. She can sing 'straight' when she wants to – there are many examples of fine, relatively faithful melody readings in her canon. But one suspects that when she chooses to 'bend' a tune it is rather less to do with the quality of the material she is singing and more with how she 'feels'; that could be, by turns, adventurous and inspired or inebriated and plain tired. Sometimes, doing anything other than what came easily, i.e, her 'own way of doing it', might have just been too much effort. Consequently, it doesn't always come off.

The infamous 28 straight A's in 'I'll Get By' (1937) cannot help but wear the listener down, while Gunther Schuller cites 'I Can't Get Started' (1938) as an inappropriate and unsuccessful example of Billie's recomposition methods, pointing to her flattening of Vernon Duke's melody ('one of the finest tunes of the decade') into 'something much less imaginative'.

Commentators of the journalistic and musicological schools often draw on each other's insights in the pursuit of the essence of Billie Holiday's art, though there is a sense that in Billie's case, musical analysis is a limited tool. Benny Green is deeply suspicious of the 'diabolonian cunning' of theorists who discuss instinctive jazz in mathematical terms, asserting that in the case of Holiday 'there is nothing to compute, no inversions to detect, no daring passing chords to recognize by name, none of the contents of the usual box of vocal tricks which may easily be defined according to the rules of discord and resolution.' And though Gunther Schuller's work is full of illuminating and insightful observations concerning the musical, tonal and emotional detail of Billie's music, broadly (and interestingly) he agrees with Green.

Schuller (with my italics): 'It is a truism to regard Billie Holiday as one of the great artists of jazz. But her art transcends the usual categorizations of style, content, and technique. Much of her singing goes beyond itself and becomes a *humanistic document;* it passed often into a realm that is not only *beyond criticism* but in the deepest sense *inexplicable.* We can, of course, describe and analyse the surface mechanics of her art: her style, her techniques, her personal vocal attributes; and I suppose a poet could express the essence of her art or at least give us, by poetic analogy, his particular insight into it. But, as with all truly profound art, that which operates above, below, and all around its outer manifestations is what most touches us, and also remains *ultimately mysterious.*'

'Mysterious' is a word that even the most thorough of analysts resort to, especially in relation to Billie Holiday's free-floating rhythmic conception. Barry Kernfeld goes to some trouble to illustrate her 'fluid and fixed, premeditated and spontaneous' paraphrasing technique before observing, with my italics, 'her use of leaping grace notes and sliding blues notes further heightens the *mystery* of precise rhythmic placement'.

For Hao and Rachel Huang, however, it is not enough to talk of the 'elusive something' in Billie's rhythmic 'declamation, which seems somehow suspended in time'. They embark on an earnest investigation ('by means of a little tedious arithmetic' and a 'spatial grid') that 'proves' the 'dual-track time' in Billie's music, i.e., that 'there are two beat systems functioning simultaneously, one governing the accompaniment and the other regulating the vocal line.' That these beat systems are also 'unsynchronised' means they exist in a 'shifting limbo'. However, although 'the two parallel strands organising the passage of time might be irreconcilable, [they] yet must be grasped simultaneously' because 'this is the profound conceptual challenge of Billie's art'.

Conceptual challenges apart, Gary Giddins, respected jazz critic of the *Village Voice*, also suggests that the 'language of musical technique' can only take us so far toward an understanding of her art because musicology 'doesn't suggest the primary impact of her singing, which is emotional'. Giddings observes that 'despite a thin voice and a range of about 15 notes, she overpowered musicians and listeners with multi-layered nuances...Bessie Smith and Louis Armstrong adapted blues and improvisational devices to pop songs, but it was Holiday who pushed their achievement into the realm of unmitigated intimacy.'

Part of that intimacy was her sound ('rather a shock when one hears if for the first time,' as Martin Williams puts it), which writers wrestle to describe, often resorting to Schuller's 'poetic analogy'. Feather talks of her 'tart, gritty timbre', Gleason of her voice of 'sulphur-and-molasses', Schuller of her 'olive-toned timbre' and 'infinitely subtle shadings and timbral nuances' like her 'lilting, rolling "l"', her 'stretching "I"', 'bright-hued "aaah"s' and the 'enhancing...giddy-light' quality of her 'hoarseness'. Little wonder it was said that no one sang 'hunger' or 'yearning' or 'love' the way Billie Holiday did.

As the relative merits of the different phases of her career, the received wisdom is that the Columbia-era sides have a fresh invention and vitality that is quashed by the pop sides of the Decca era, with the 1950s sides being well-meaning but low-achieving and the Ellis albums a sorry finale. Broadly speaking, it is a sustainable view but one that is proposed generally by jazz commentators, who naturally regard the work of Billie Holiday, Great Jazz Singer as their province.

One of the standard claims for Billie's early work is that her advanced melodic and rhythmic variations on run-of-the-mill material had a base-metal-into-gold quality. Schuller, however, is not so sure about the 'triumph over the material' angle, regarding it as a cliché of the 'insular...supreme and unassailable' tastes of jazz critics. Will Friedwald is even more forthright in his book *Jazz Singing*: 'Listen, folks, those one-shot songs that Billie Holiday does are wonderful. Even party-line purists who don't care for pop, big bands, Broadway, or Busby Berkeley have to admit that Tin Pan Alley...was one of the greatest friends jazz ever had, no less than the blues. Sure, Holiday improves on them, but no more than she does "They Can't Take That Away From Me" or "The Man I Love"or the way she turns standard blues material into performances as special as "Billie's Blues".'

Friedwald and (to some extent) Schuller also depart somewhat from the general sense – represented here by Williams's view – that the Decca period was 'stilted' and 'did not encourage her former melodic and emotional freedom'. Friedwald regards the Decca tenure 'despite a few middle-brow misfires' as 'the most entertaining and polished in her whole career. Surprises abound in this underappreciated period'. Schuller observes that contrary to critics 'lauding her ability to prevail' over the choice of backing, 'Billie seems clearly energised and inspired by these accompaniments...she seems to be feeding on the ideas contained in the arrangements'. Like the criticism dished out to Charlie Parker's with-strings recordings (of which he was proud, as Billie was of hers), the tastes of jazz critics seem to be at odds not only with later commentators with a broader aesthetic, but also with the artists themselves.

Critical confusion continues in relation to Billie's later work but it is not so easily delineated into a jazz/pop divide; the response to the sound of a great expressive artist losing control of her instrument of expression appears to be a profoundly personal one, with responses ranging from disinterest to deep uneasiness, to depression and catharsis. Green insists that the last of Billie Holiday's work must be 'accepted as recitative with musical accompaniment rather than just ordinary singing,' and that it should not be played to anyone 'unaware of the details of the life and career of the singer'. If one keeps in mind 'her handling of a lyric' the last recordings are 'not the insufferable croakings of a woman already half-dead, but recitatives whose dramatic intensity becomes unbearable, statements as frank and tragic as anything throughout the whole range of popular art.'

Stuart Nicholson agrees that 'it is necessary to know Billie's real-life history to interpret the album properly. As one half of the mind struggles and reacts to the boozy huskiness in her voice and her shaky intonation, the other half listens, searching for meaning in both voice and lyrics. This disjunction produces an extremely uncomfortable listening experience'. Most commentators, however, whether it is to their taste or not, refer to what Schuller calls her 'emotionally overwhelming singing' of this period, but once more we are back to the idea that in order to fully appreciate Billie Holiday's music, we must *know* Billie Holiday's story.

However, if you really want to know how good Billie Holiday was, ask a musician. Of the many who knew and worked with Billie, it is perhaps the pianists who are in a unique position to offer their perspective on Billie's gifts. Her partner from their great music of the thirties, Teddy Wilson, is in the minority in his expressed reserve concerning her abilities. 'I was much more excited by the musicians we had on those dates that I was about Billie...[she] was not a particular favourite of mine.' Wilson even downplays the individuality of her style, pointing to her influences. 'To me Billie was like a girl doing a take-off on Louis Armstrong. It was novel, no one else had thought to do it, but I didn't think it was original.'

Although appearing to be genuinely unenthusiastic about Billie's singing (preferring the clear-voiced, straightforward approach of singers like Baby White), this could be taken as a curmudgeonly response to all the attention she subsequently received, even on records with Wilson's name at the top. However, as it stands, it represents the view of those (and there are a few) who regarded Billie Holiday's reputation as out of proportion to her legacy.

The vast majority of other pianists are generous and genuinely respectful of her musical talents. Johnny Guarnieri, who played with her at the Onyx in the 1940s, called her 'the greatest tempo singer that ever lived'. Bobby Tucker, lifelong friend and accompanist 1947–49 agrees: 'Wherever I put the tune she found the groove and made it happen. She could swing in the hardest tempo and float on top of it like it was made for her; when I put it slow, she sang slow – but the most beautiful slow you ever heard.'

Tucker has often talked of Billie's insecurity in her own abilities: 'She never thought too much of herself as a singer anyway. She thought of herself more as an extension of a jazz horn.' However, he also remembers her personal presence: 'It was never a matter of playing an intro until the audience quietened down. She had the whole thing…she had your attention, from right "now".'

Jimmy Rowles, who after first seeing her in a California club as a 'little punk piano player of twenty-two', in 1942 admitted that 'by the end of that first night I was in love with her'. When they got around to making music together 'I loved playing for her. It was *rare*…She was part of the music. That's why everybody loved her. She wasn't just a singer. She was *there*.'

Oscar Peterson confessed to not being a fan until he realised her rhythmic capabilities and by the time of their first recording session, found himself 'just snowed under by what she was doing…She'd just sing her own time and somehow it happened to match. It was unbelievable. She could go way out there and then she'd come back in a way that you wouldn't expect. Suddenly she'd be standing there beside you'.

Mal Waldron, her final accompanist, 1957–59, makes much of her credentials as a jazz musician, pointing to how she would prepare a song. 'When she took up a tune, she felt it the way a jazz musician would. She'd get the piano player to play it down a few times, and she'd listen to the tune, and she'd get an overall approach to the tune, and she sang it as a "whole". She didn't work on it bar by bar, the way most singers do. Jazz musicians think of a tune in terms of a unit, a sequence, how it moves; you have to, if you're going to solo on it. That's how she heard a tune.'

Although he was her musical partner in her traumatic final years, Waldron remembers that 'the young Billie had more energy but the old Billie had more experience. Sure the voice was going, but the emotion and the *spirit* were as strong as ever.' Reiterating Rowles's and Tucker's experience, Waldron says 'it wasn't like playing for a singer, it was like playing for another horn. Because she responded to everything like a jazz musician…She was a natural talent…It takes time to go to school; it takes time away from living that life that you're living which is really responsible for the music you're singing.'

The final few words of appreciation should come from that group of people over whom Billie Holiday had perhaps the deepest and most lasting influence, the singers that followed and learned from her.

On Billie Holiday's emotional impact, Shirley Horn, jazz ballad singer-pianist: 'Billie Holiday could make you feel everything she was feeling. Whatever she was feeling. There's few singers can do that.' Helen Merrill, jazz singer: 'When she sang something, it touched a universal button.'

On Billie Holiday's influence, Helen Merrill: 'You can't do anything about becoming "her". A lot of singers tried. And a lot went into drugs and things, thinking that's what would make them sing better.' Abbey Lincoln, powerful, emotionally charged jazz singer: 'So many singers copy the mannerisms, rather than the essence, the musicality.'

On Billie Holiday's craft, Diana Krall: 'A musician's singer… it was her musicianship, her artistry which was so important.'

Tony Bennett: 'No one seems to know that craft any more. She was a great teacher.'

And finally, an acknowledgement of debt from the man who for many is the ultimate jazz-pop singer and the greatest musical communicator of the 20th century vernacular arts, Frank Sinatra: 'With a few exceptions, every major pop singer in the US during her generation has been touched in some way by her genius. It is Billie Holiday whom I first heard in 52nd Street clubs in the early thirties, who was, and remains the greatest single musical influence on me.'

BIBLIOGRAPHY

Wishing On The Moon: The Life And Times Of Billie Holiday
   by Donald Clarke (Viking)
Billie Holiday by Stuart Nicholson (Victor Gollancz)
The Billie Holiday Companion by Leslie Gourse (Omnibus)
Billie's Blues: The True Story Of The Immortal Billie Holiday
   by John Chilton (Quartet)
Lady Sings The Blues by Billie Holiday with William Dufty
   (Penguin)
The Swing Era by Gunther Schuller (Oxford University Press)
What To Listen For In Jazz by Barry Kernfeld (Yale University
   Press)
Jazz Voices by Kitty Grime (Quartet)
Singing Jazz by Bruce Crowther and Mike Pinfold (Blandford)
Annual Review Of Jazz Studies 7 edited by Dan Morgenstern
   et al (Scarecrow Press for the Institute Of Jazz Studies,
   Rutgers University, New Jersey)
The Jazz Tradition by Martin Williams (Oxford University
   Press)
The Reluctant Art by Benny Green (McGibbon and Kay)
Jazz Singing by Will Friedwald (Quartet)
The Best Of Jazz by Humphrey Lyttleton (Robson Books)
The Jazz Years by Leonard Feather (Quartet)
Good Morning Blues by Count Basie with Albert Murray
   (Paladin)

Hear Me Talkin' To Ya by Nat Shapiro and Nat Hentoff (Souvenir)

New Grove Dictionary Of Jazz edited by Barry Kernfeld (Macmillan)

Penguin Guide To Jazz by Brian Morton and Richard Cook (Penguin)

Complete Billie Holiday On Verve Sleeve Notes by Phil Schapp and Joel E Siegal

Complete Decca Recordings Sleeve Notes by Stephen Lasker

The Quintessential Billie Holiday Sleeve Notes by Michael Brooks

Issues of jazz periodicals *Down Beat*, *Jazz Time* and *Jazz Journal*

INDEX

PICTURE CREDITS

Picture section page 1: © The 50s Collection/Retna Ltd. 2 top: Pictorial Press Ltd; bottom Hulton Getty. 3 top and bottom: Michael Ochs Archives/Redferns. 4 top and bottom: Pictorial Press Ltd. 5 top and bottom: Pictorial Press Ltd. 6 top and bottom: Hulton Getty. 7 top: Bob Willoughby/Redferns; bottom: Pictorial Press Ltd. 8: Pictorial Press Ltd.

ACKNOWLEDGEMENTS

Thank you. For professional support – Sharon Kelly at Sony Jazz, Julie Allison at Universal Jazz, Kerstan Mackness at VIA and Martin Aston at Editing Central. For calling me in '89 – Jim Irvin. For musical nourishment – Kevin, Andy, Rob, Russ, Mike and Phil. For everything – all my love to Tracy, Polly and Alexander at Moodswing Manor.